LISA H.

LISA H.

THE TRUE STORY OF
AN EXTRAORDINARY AND
COURAGEOUS WOMAN

Richard Severo

HARPER & ROW, PUBLISHERS, New York
Cambridge, Philadelphia, San Francisco, London
Mexico City, São Paulo, Singapore, Sydney

1817

*This book is for Thomas
and Mary Severo*

The poem on page 120 is reprinted by permission. The name of the copyright holder is omitted here by request.

LISA H. Copyright © 1985 by Richard Severo. All rights reserved. Printed in the United States of America. No part of this book may be used or reproduced in any manner whatsoever without written permission except in the case of brief quotations embodied in critical articles and reviews. For information address Harper & Row, Publishers, Inc., 10 East 53rd Street, New York, N.Y. 10022. Published simultaneously in Canada by Fitzhenry & Whiteside Limited, Toronto.

FIRST EDITION

Designer: Sidney Feinberg

Library of Congress Cataloging in Publication Data

Severo, Richard.
  Lisa H. : the true story of an extraordinary and
courageous woman.

  1. Neurofibromatosis—Patients—United States—
Biography. I. Title.
RC280.N4S48 1985   362.1'9699383 [B]   84-48193
ISBN 0-06-015405-4

85 86 87 88 10 9 8 7 6 5 4 3 2 1

Acknowledgments

It won't be possible to thank by name all of the key people who helped make this book possible. Not because I don't remember them, but because Lisa's desire to remain anonymous is a reasonable one and I respect it. And so while I must thank Lisa, her family and friends for memories they patiently shared with me in many long talks, I can't tell you their real identities, even though it is they who will tell you Lisa's story in the chapters to come.

I can mention two people, whom you will meet, and whose real names I have used, because they cannot so easily be linked to Lisa. They are Verna Mitros, the friend whose desire to help Lisa led her to Linton A. Whitaker, M.D., Lisa's principal plastic surgeon; and Robert Thompson, her sixth grade teacher. He remains, in her memory, a man who gave her his friendship at a time when many others around her would not.

The original idea for the articles I wrote about Lisa that appeared in *The New York Times* and other newspapers came from Shay McConnell, a public relations representative for the Hospital of the University of Pennsylvania. Inviting a reporter to witness radical surgery, carrying with it a fair risk of a less-than-successful result, is not the sort of thing public relations specialists for hospitals are supposed to do. But Shay did it, did it well and continued to help me after a friend, Peter

Stamelman, convinced me that I should write this book. Shay's continued trust in me, her unfailing honesty and sense of professionalism—and her own interest in Lisa—helped make the task easier and the end product better.

I am no less indebted to the hospital, its administration, its physicians and its other workers who also trusted me and extended to me many courtesies. Among them, Mark Levitan, who then served as executive director; Edward Stemmler, M.D., Dean of the School of Medicine, University of Pennsylvania; Dr. Whitaker, whose skill and audacity made the operation a reality; James Katowitz, M.D., Lisa's ophthalmic plastic surgeon, whose skills and compassion as a teacher and friend rival his ability in the operating room; and Derek Bruce, M.D., a neurosurgeon, who unexpectedly played such a pivotal role in her surgery.

Others associated with the Hospital of the University of Pennsylvania who gave of their time, wisdom and cooperation were Peter Randall, M.D., and Harold G. Scheie, M.D., who operated on Lisa when she was very young; Ellen Jantzen, M.D., John Lecky, M.D., anesthesiologists; Donato LaRossa, M.D., microsurgeon; Michael Pertschuk, M.D., psychiatrist; James Zins, M.D., and Eric Blomain, M.D., plastic surgeons.

Among the operating room nurses, I must thank, and express my admiration for: Joyce Carr, Joan Widua, William Jackson, Carlena Saunders, and Karen Scheidigg. Other nurses who helped Lisa after surgery included Jackie Lydon, Eileen McAleer, Linda Hartranft and Michelle Howardell.

Still others at the hospital who contributed to this book were Elaine Stevens, Lois Carita, and Gloria Iannone. Special thanks also to Mrs. Renata Whitaker, for her hospitality and for her own insights into what Lisa's case was about.

I had much difficulty, in the beginning of this project, in understanding the nature of the cruelty that was inflicted on Lisa. I therefore sought and received much expert help in understanding the shunning to which Lisa and so many other handicapped people are subjected.

I am indebted to Dr. Ashley Montagu, whose own original research into the life of the Elephant Man educated me and inspired me and who found the time to further enlighten me as I wrote about Lisa. I also received more professional help in understanding discrimination in its present and historic forms through the efforts of David Forrest, M.D., Columbia Presbyterian Medical Center; James Masterson, M.D., Cornell Medical School; Robert Murray, Ph.D., and James Leach, Colgate University; and Michael Baden, M.D., former chief medical examiner of New York.

Still others who gave me lucid and varied thoughts on how to write Lisa's story were Penny Aviles, Suzanne Donner, Lynn Courtemanche, Peter Barrett, Robert and Kathryn Boyle, Andrea Troy, Jennifer Dunning, Mary Jane Curley, Jim Delihas, Andrea Smith, Lewis Milford, Jed Mattes, Anne and David Seymour, Joan Cook, Harry Fisdell, Robert Tanenbaum, Mab Salinger Gray, Gene Ruffini, and Barbara L. Kaplan.

Also of invaluable help in this regard were Joan Rudd, president of the National Neurofibromatosis Foundation; Felice Yahr, the Foundation's executive director; Rita Kasky, former executive director; Allan E. Rubenstein, M.D., chairman of the Foundation's Medical Advisory Board; William Baum, of the Foundation's chapter in southeastern Pennsylvania; members of the Foundation's Metropolitan Washington, D.C., chapter; Penny Schwartz, social work consultant to the Foundation; and to the members of the neurofibromatosis group at Mount Sinai Medical Center in New York City.

My understanding of the enormity of the scientific challenge posed by neurofibromatosis was enhanced by talks with Mrs. Yahr and Dr. Rubenstein and also with two active researchers—Arthur Bloom, M.D., Columbia University; and Catherine Mytilineou, Ph.D., Mount Sinai Medical Center.

There were many hundreds of fellow writers, some of them members of Local 3 of the Newspaper Guild or of the National Writers Union, others not affiliated with any organization or union, who gave me expressions of needed support at critical times during the book's creation, times when doubts were expressed in some quarters that it could become a reality. I want to particularly thank the Guild's Barry Lipton, Ed Egan, and Bea Eastman for their steadfastness and Phil Tobin, a Guild attorney, for his observations on any number of literary problems, all of which he helped me solve. By the same token, I specifically want to thank my friends and co-workers at *The New York Times* for their continued strong interest in the Lisa project.

Although talking to Lisa and to her family and friends was always pleasurable, writing about what happened to them was not. The constructive criticisms of my editor, Lawrence P. Ashmead, served to keep me faithful to my reportorial mission.

My wife, Emöke de Papp Severo, devoted many hours to typing what appears to be several thousand pages of transcripts, and somehow she still had the energy afterward to make many helpful comments on how to improve the telling of Lisa's story.

Introduction

Lisa H. is the pseudonym of a young contemporary woman who wanted very little out of life. Or, you might very well argue, she wanted the most precious things that life has to offer, the things we all want and must have, whoever, whatever and wherever we are.

She wanted to be liked, loved, accepted and acceptable as a human being. Not more than everyone else or less than everyone else—but just like anyone else. Her wants, therefore, seem quite reasonable. She wanted this acceptance more than all else in the world. But she was denied it because, quite simply, her face was unlike anyone else's. There was no other reason. Indeed, there were a great many reasons for people to like Lisa very much. But they did not.

Lisa sought ordinary acceptance so badly that she risked her very life to embark on an extraordinary medical adventure. Her adventure is as harrowing as it is exciting, as compelling in human terms as it is challenging scientifically and medically.

Lisa, who is a real person living near Philadelphia, suffers from a genetically determined disorder known as neurofibromatosis. It is the same disorder suffered a century ago by a good and gentle man named Joseph Merrick, also known as John Merrick, best known as the Elephant Man. But the nature of Lisa's disorder took a different form from that suffered by Merrick. The way she dealt with it was markedly different. What happened to her as a result is most different of all.

Lisa's disorder attacked her face with unusual fury, congesting it with tumors that literally buried her face—and therefore her hope to be accepted by others. Her plastic surgeon and others with whom he consulted say hers is the most severe case of facial neurofibromatosis on record. Aside from her face, she is as physically strong and active as she is warm and engaging.

Because her problem appeared as it did and where it did, Lisa H. was shunned and abused in a way that seems implausible in the twentieth century. At least it did for the people who watched it happen. It is not that the twentieth century is such a wellspring of humanism. We know that it is not. But some of us have a sufficiently high opinion of our times so that we find it hard to accept the notion that the Elephant Man's story was not just a solitary instance of unusual cruelty to a human being. We would like to think that nothing like it could ever happen again. To know Lisa and to understand what happened to her is to realize that it has happened again. And, sad to say, it will happen again and again in the future unless we humankind change.

This book covers more than twenty years of a woman's life. It has been pieced together from the recollections of people who witnessed that life, as well as from what I saw myself as a reporter.

The name "Lisa H." is the name that she asked be used for this book, to protect her privacy. Most of the names of her friends and members of her family have also been changed, for the same reason. But the names of a fine teacher whom she loved and of the physicians and other professionals who came into her life are unchanged. And the facts presented about them are true.

The setting for the book and the events described are all true, at least as true as the writer's craft and the memories and perceptions of those he interviews can be.

Lisa, who is as intensely private as she is friendly and agreeable, decided to permit me to write this book only because she hoped that the telling of her story might help many people. She asked for anonymity, I promised it, and she shall have it. I agree with her that knowledge of what she did might help people.

But what people? Surely not just people with neurofibromatosis or any other serious, physically disabling or disfiguring medical problem that causes them the pain and rejection that Lisa has known. Not just for them.

In truth, Lisa's story is for all of us.

It is for anyone who has ever wondered about beauty's power to build a life or the fearsome power of beauty's absence to devastate one;

for anyone who has wondered what it is that we humans really dislike and fear in each other and how far we may go to express that fear;

for anyone who is willing to explore the darkest sides of our souls, as well as the brightest sparkles of courage and compassion and enlightenment that distinguish the human spirit.

—RICHARD SEVERO

New York
February 1985

Chapter One

I knocked on Lisa's door. There was no answer, at least not right away. I stood there on her front porch, waiting to meet her for the very first time.

It was a soft, gray-yellow November afternoon, and the time was precisely three o'clock, the time we had set for our meeting in a brief but amicable telephone conversation. She had sounded much younger than her twenty-one years.

The weather was mild, agreeable, even though the prelude of a winter sky was trying with some success to hide the sun. Autumn was seven weeks old and Thanksgiving was less than three weeks away, but it did not seem that way. That is the way November can be in Lisa's part of Pennsylvania.

Her neighborhood looked peaceful enough, viewed quickly and for the first time from her front porch. Exuberant rose bushes had been clipped and tied, readied for winter, one homeowner nearby had already put a buff burlap snow cover over his rhododendrons, and the oak across the street that Lisa had climbed years before with a girl named Nancy had already been stripped of its golden brown leaves by chill of lengthening nights. But I knew nothing of Nancy, nor of the great oak, nor of rose bushes barren, waiting for first snow.

There was a stirring behind the weathered door and it opened. There was Lisa. "Hello," she said in her little-girl

1

voice, a voice seeming more hesitant now than it had on the telephone.

That was reasonable; I had come to talk to Lisa about her face. Her face was not a pleasant thing for her to consider. She would not look at her face in the mirror. Why should she want to talk to a stranger about it?

I looked at Lisa's face for the first time. Enormous tumors hung from both sides of it. They swooped downward, thick stalks of flesh that obliterated the ends of her mouth. She really had no nose, in the sense that most people think of a nose. There was no profile, nothing more than a lumpy mass that lacked projection, shape. Her brows were thick, gnarled, engulfed in tumor. There was tumor everywhere, it seemed; massive tumor all over her face, reaching from her eyes back toward her ears and along her lower left jaw. There was so much tumor that the weight of it had pulled the skin on her face downward, so that the openings for her eyes had drooped, making it hard to see much of her eyes. It was as though her face had been cast in wax as the theater's traditional mask of tragedy, then worsened, as if the wax were melting from fierce fire, pulling her eyes downward, pulling her mouth downward, burying her eyes and her mouth in tumor.

Later, people would ask me what I felt like in that first moment and I would not know what to tell them. I was not obsessed with her face, nor riveted by it, nor repulsed, nor angry, nor frightened. I only thought that it was unfair that she or anyone should have such a face.

She was a small young woman, perhaps five feet tall, not much more. She opened the door wider and beckoned me to enter. There was a modestly proportioned living room immediately beyond the door, filled with all manner of objects, indicating that someone in the house spent a lot of time collecting. The collection was eclectic: some of the objects were there for amusement, not beauty; others had a certain grace; still others looked as if they were shrewdly purchased bargains; all of them together made the place more comfortable, at least for an unrepentant collector. There was a little radio inside a model of a Rolls-Royce, there was a brass reading lamp, there was also a pine desk. On an étagère in the corner, lots of interesting things were lined up: eggs made of mahogany, obsidian, and onyx; a porcelain bird; a rabbit that looked as if it had been made of marble. And there were other little things wrought of glass, metal or wood from Yugoslavia, Taiwan, Holland and Brazil. I saw some hand-painted Italian flowerpots and a rather handsome handmade cabinet that I supposed was American. In that house, it was all American.

Nobody else was home. Lisa's welcome had been friendly enough but now she was silent, and she sat down on the couch across from me, waiting for me to say whatever it was I had to say. I fished through my blue canvas knapsack, found a worn manila folder and from it took a Xerox copy of an article I had written for *The New York Times* in 1980, captioned "DESPITE CONTROVERSY, 100,000 ANNUALLY OPT FOR HEART OPERATION," with a subheadline that said, "One Man's Ordeal Typifies Experience of Bypass Surgery." The man's name was Everton Kirkland and, as a science writer, I had attended his open-heart surgery at the University of Alabama, to the apparent satisfaction of my editors, who reasoned that perhaps I had the fortitude to watch other kinds of surgery as well.

Lisa was going to have another kind of surgery—a surgery unprecedented and radical, a surgery that would try to remove the disfiguring tumors that I saw before me. I did not know much about it, but if I were going to be permitted to witness it, as my editors wished, then I would have to get Lisa's permission. She wasn't so sure my presence in the operating room was what she wanted.

"If you'll read it over," I told Lisa in my best reportorial earnestness, "you'll see that it is informative, and I'd like to take much the same approach with your surgery, if you'll let me."

"I don't know," she said, promising that she would read the article. "I've already told Dr. Whitaker that I don't want my name in the newspaper. I am a private person. I'd like to be in the woodwork. The only reason I would have for doing this is if I thought it might help other people who are going through the same thing."

Then more silence. Obviously, she wasn't going to permit me to attend her surgery if she didn't trust me and she wasn't sure about that yet.

We started to talk. At least, I did. I asked her the obvious, soft, nonprobing questions reporters ask when they don't want to frighten away an interview, and she gave me the obvious, soft, nonrevealing answers of one already frightened, ready to bolt. She switched on a tape recorder. I asked her what her major was in college and she said she had started out as a speech major and originally wanted to work with children who had impaired hearing, but she wasn't so sure about that now. She wasn't sure about much of anything now. She still liked children. But she wasn't entirely sure if they liked her. Or if anybody at all liked her.

Lisa had a genetically caused disorder called neurofibromatosis. That is the more recent nomenclature for what used to be called von Recklinghausen's Disease, named after Frederick Daniel von Recklinghausen, the nineteenth-century German pathologist who first described it in an 1882 monograph. But except for physicians, most people who are aware of the condition at all tend to think of it as the Elephant Man's Disease, because it is irrevocably linked to Joseph Merrick, also called John Merrick, who was dubbed "the Elephant Man" and who became famous as such when Londoners became aware of him, on display, as an "attraction" in a shop in the Mile End Road, near London Hospital. The practice of calling neurofibromatosis "Elephant Man's Disease" is offensive to a great many of the people who have it, who feel that it theatricalizes and thus trivializes a problem of tragic proportions.

Merrick was first the subject of a compassionate monograph written by his physician and benefactor, Sir Frederick Treves, and first published in 1923, thirty-three years after Merrick's death; then of a learned explanation of his personal qualities and experiences by Ashley Montagu, published in 1971; later, of an award-winning play by Bernard Pomerance; and also of an acclaimed motion picture, written by Christopher DeVore, Eric Bergen and David Lynch. With all of it, I still did not know very much about Merrick; but the notion of a disease so totally associated with the look of bestiality seemed darkly ancient, remote to the point of witchery, improbable in an age of medical enlightenment. If the deformity from which Merrick suffered was not a make-believe disease, surely such an abomination of a sickness would not so soon be repeated, not in a time when genetic research was pursued so aggressively and successfully; surely the extraordinary barbarity to which he was subjected in the soot-dank and narrow cobbled streets of post-Dickensian England would not be repeated, a century later, in the suburban, automoted and automated Philadelphia of the 1980s. The Merrick that Treves knew had been "dragged from town to town and from fair to fair as if he were a strange beast in a cage." He was shunned, beaten, so totally abused by humankind that Treves wrote that what Merrick most dreaded "were the open street and the gaze of his fellow-men." That, I was sure, could not possibly happen again.

I insisted upon my own doubts even though I knew that Ashley Montagu was an anthropologist and social biologist, not a writer of fiction. And yet, even within his scholarly restraint and his lucid effort to explain the genetic mutation that had been Merrick's calamity, there seemed to be only the phantom of an illness that could not happen again.

But it had happened again. Merrick's case, among the worst ever seen, involved large parts of his face and body. Lisa suffered the deformity of large tumors only on her face, but over all of it, where the deformity is there for all to see and to judge. The skin elsewhere on her body had been infiltrated with neurofibromas but they had not developed into visible tumors.

On that first day when I met Lisa, she spoke of neurofibromatosis as if it were nothing more than a persistent case of poison ivy.

"Do you think the disease is still progressing?" I asked her.

"I don't know. Probably."

"Has your face changed in the past year?"

"I don't know, really. I never look at my face."

"Why not? Do you find it disagreeable?"

"Yes."

"There is more than one way to measure beauty."

"You can't prove that to me. If you are shopping and someone passes a comment, what good are the other standards for measuring beauty?"

"Perhaps you'll reach a point where derisive comments won't bother you so much."

"Maybe. I certainly haven't reached it yet."

"What advantages do you think you'll get out of surgery?"

"Improvement."

"Improvement? What kind of improvement?"

"Well, I don't think I'm going to look like Farrah Fawcett. I know for sure that's not going to happen. But I'd want to have this surgery if there were only one percent improvement."

"One percent? You are taking great risks for one percent."

"Yes. I realize that my face might be permanently paralyzed if they cut the wrong nerves."

"What will you do if there is some paralysis?"

"No problem. It beats looking like this."

There was awkward silence.

"Do you like music?" The question was an old standby. I used it whenever I thought I'd run out of things to ask.

She brightened. "Music? Yes. I like music very much."

She excused herself, went upstairs and brought back the only classical album she had: Bach's Brandenburg Concertos no. 2 and no. 6 and the Clavier Concerto in D Minor, as presented by Funk & Wagnalls' Family Library of Great Music. It had been on special at a grocery store for 99 cents.

"I can't tell you where the woodwinds leave off and the strings begin," she said, "but Bach is good thinking music."

Then we began to talk of many things—of Brahms (she liked

his "Lullaby"), of Haydn (she did not like the "Surprise Symphony" very much and wasn't sure why), of Engelbert Humperdinck (not the late-nineteenth-century German composer who wrote the opera *Hansel and Gretel*, but rather the extant pop music singer), of Johnny Mathis and Nat King Cole and The Beatles.

She also liked spaghetti, Ukrainian and Chinese food, latch-hook rugs, paintings of sunrises and sunsets. "But I don't have any special artist that I like," she said.

She had a weakness for castles, and on occasion would go to the County Jail in Norristown, just to look at it, because it represented her idea of how a British castle should appear. She liked British history ("castles, damsels in distress, the whole bit"); Stonehenge ("it's neat"), the pyramids and the Sphinx. She liked American thought and culture from the late 1600s on and was interested in history generally, "if it's not boring."

We also talked of friendships.

"I don't have a whole lot of friends my own age," she said, "and my sister Diane is my best friend. I am very lucky. I have three very good sisters. But Diane is special to me; I can talk to her about anything."

The afternoon wore on and now I found myself in no particular hurry to leave. By the time two hours had passed, she represented something totally "normal" to me, if I may be permitted the reluctant but convenient use of that atrociously ambiguous and hopelessly unkind word; I had to make myself remember that there was any affliction at all.

In college, she told me, she had reached the junior level but had taken the fall semester off because of the December operation, now less than six weeks away. And by the radical nature of it, she'd miss the spring semester, too. We talked easily and she then began, uneasily, to tell me some of the things that had happened to her.

It had not occurred to me that anything extraordinary would have happened to her. As a child, like the other children I grew up with, I had been taught not to stare nor to take delight in someone else's misery. That lesson was so basic, so easy to learn, that I had assumed, foolishly, that almost everybody else in the world had been taught the same lesson. She corrected me. In her view, too many had not. And the problem was much greater than one of stares and double takes.

There were tears streaming down her troubled, tortured face as she told me about her neighbor, a middle-class man who lived a few doors away with his wife and son. This was a man who had lived there for some years, had watched her face gradually disappear under tumor, had seen the pain it caused her and her family.

He knew these things and on Halloween night, not long before my visit, he brought his son to Lisa's house, trick or treating. Lisa's father, Harry, was home, in the kitchen, watching television. He always found Halloween something of a nuisance and he had no intention of answering the door. Lisa had not shared his indifference to Halloween and other holidays. She loved children, loved to see them in their costumes and masks, hear their satisfied cooing when she gave them candy. That was the reason that Mary, Lisa's mother, saw to it that the house contained a good supply of Tootsie Pops. Lisa answered the door and Harry continued to watch television in the kitchen.

She recognized her neighbors and welcomed them, then went into the kitchen to get the little boy his candy. When she returned to the living room, the boy's father pointed at Lisa and chuckled, "Boy, isn't that a skit? *Look at that scary mask.*"

The boy, candy in hand, did not seem to understand what it was all about as his father led him out into the black autumn night, a night filled with happiness and laughter beyond the yellow glow from the front porches on the block, the laughter of neighbors sharing a Halloween with their children. Beyond the yellow glow, the man laughed with his son in the darkness with his friends and neighbors. As he went, he was surely pleased that he had been able to share an amusing moment with his son.

That Halloween night, Lisa went upstairs to her little room at the rear of the house, overlooking the backyard, and wept softly, keeping her tears to herself. This sort of thing had happened to her before, and when it did she almost always went alone to her room at the rear of the house, there to weep alone. That night, she did not tell her father what had happened. Other members of her family found out about it much later. She seldom told them about such things. She had taught herself not to. It only upset them. And Lisa knew that there was nothing, really, that they could do to stop it.

As for the little boy, he immediately developed into one of Lisa's tormentors, not missing an opportunity to point her out when one of his friends from another neighborhood visited him.

In the week that had elapsed, he had come to enjoy approaching her from behind, when she was walking her dog. Once, she heard him say to his friends, "Now watch, I'll say hello to her and you can take a quick look to see how ugly she is."

Her family never said anything to either the boy or his father. She told me this and it was as if we had entered a time machine, more powerful than Jules Verne's. When we did, Merrick was not so far away, after all. His dread was her dread. But this was the present and I felt myself losing my reportorial objectivity, fighting the suggestion that something I had regarded as almost mythic that had happened in the shadows of London streets a century before could happen now.

It was not an isolated incident. After Halloween had passed, she was in a shopping center and there was another man with another son.

"A little late for Halloween, isn't it?" he asked her with a mocking laugh. The little boy stared at her.

On another occasion, in a restaurant at the Strawbridge & Clothier store in Plymouth Meeting, a middle-aged woman loudly complained to Mary, who was then a waitress there, "Look at that. Look at *that*. People who look like her should not be allowed in here."

"She is my daughter," Mary said.

"I don't care who she is," the woman answered. "She

shouldn't be allowed. People like her shouldn't be allowed. You shouldn't have brought her in here. You had no right."

Once, Lisa and Mary were in the clothing department of the same store and another woman screamed, "They ought to put her in a cage."

This time, Mary didn't have to say anything. The saleswoman had known both Mary and Lisa for a long time, loved them both, and spent the next several minutes telling the surprised woman that the customer wasn't always right, at least not in that department, that it was a vicious and evil thing to say and that perhaps she ought to shop elsewhere, and do it soon. The customer wandered off, miffed, mumbling her intention to see the management of the store about the quality of its surly, ill-mannered help. The threat of such a complaint did not bother the saleswoman and there were quite a few other salespeople at Strawbridge & Clothier who felt that way about Mary and Lisa.

For Lisa, the scalpel had thus become an imperative and she did not fear it; it was the only way she thought she had of obtaining her privilege to be a real person, acceptable not only as a friend but as a customer, as a passerby, as a pedestrian in a crowded street.

"I know I'll be all right," she told me. "I'm not afraid of the actual surgery. What I am afraid of is going up to the operating room and being put on the table. I know I'll be fine but I have these tiny fears. I know it's stupid, but I do not want to see the tops of the doors go by as I'm being wheeled up there. And I'm afraid of them leaving me in the hallway next to the operating room. Once they give me a needle, I know I'll be all right."

"Do you have a high tolerance for pain?"

"As a matter of fact, it's low. I always get Novocaine when I go to the dentist."

"If you went through this surgery and withstood all of the pain that it must entail, and then you got to the end of it and there wasn't much improvement, how would you feel?"

"I'd be a little disappointed, but it would still be worth it. I have something of an inferiority complex that needs fixing. I know I'm not inferior, but I have an inferiority complex."

We finished our chat. Lisa walked me back out to the car. The sun was setting and the sky was becoming leaden, menacing, although it was still not cold enough to snow. I had ninety-five miles to drive.

"You'll have to keep my name out of the paper," she said. "I guess it'll be O.K. if you do that." She seemed to want to talk more and so did I, but there would be plenty of time later on, now that she had agreed to my attending the surgery. She walked slowly back to the house.

I began to pick my way northward through tiny Pennsylvania villages. It suddenly seemed much colder than it probably was and the devil's hearth was reflected in the delirium of the orange and purple autumn twilight to the west of me.

The little macadam roads twisted and turned to the Pennsylvania Turnpike, which I followed eastward to the Jersey Turnpike. Yellow starbursts of light screamed toward me and blood-red lights swarmed away from me, weaving, swirling above the stink of the road like angry mosquitos. I felt curiously unprepared for the Jersey Turnpike that night: not combative enough to deal with the blur of humanity there or at the other end of it, in New York.

Chapter Two

Several weeks went by before I saw Lisa again. The next time we met it was in Examining Room No. 9 at the Hospital of the University of Pennsylvania in Philadelphia. It was to be her last major physical examination before the surgery that was supposed to give her a new face. There had been a number of physicals before, but this one was the last, the most important. Although the operation was still two weeks away, to her this examination would represent her last chance to say no. She was not the sort of person who changed her mind at the last minute. It was also the last chance her surgeons would have to express any doubts about what they had proposed, including the right to say that such a thing was not possible, after all. There was a bit of dramaturgy about the whole proceeding, a scene that threatened to overpower the calculated audacity that is preparation for creative surgery. A girl was born with a face that was unacceptable, even repugnant to much of the only world that she knew, and so her surgeon said he would give her another face, a new face fashioned from the ruins of the old one.

There had always been magic in plastic surgery and there was something unreal building now. I watched plans for an extraordinary surgery taking shape before my eyes and it seemed to me that if this succeeded, Lisa's plastic surgeon, Linton Whitaker, might be regarded as something of a sorcerer. The task he set out for himself simply did not appear possible.

Taut, quiet, Lisa sat on a little blue plastic chair at one end of the examining room, under a bright light, not really wanting to be there, not really wanting to be anyplace else in the world. Whitaker sat before her and looked intently at her face, as he had so often before in the past six months. He had never seen a face quite like it. He had admitted to me that no other face had so dominated his thinking on what the role of the plastic surgeon could be, nor caused him to wonder if he really had the skill to deal with the problems that lie upon it and within it.

It was not just the visible disfigurement that was of concern to Whitaker; Lisa's nonaesthetic medical problems were just as formidable. He knew, from his own examinations and from those of colleagues, including Dr. James Katowitz, an ophthalmic plastic surgeon, Dr. Derek Bruce, a neurosurgeon, and Dr. Rosario Mayro, an orthodontist, that tumor had invaded her skull, frontally, as well as her jaw. It had also infiltrated both of her eyes and the receptor cells behind them, causing almost total blindness in the left eye. In the right eye, vision was impaired mostly because of a cataract and glaucoma. Indeed, there had been evidence of cataracts and glaucoma in both eyes. The cataracts were part of the legacy of no less than eleven surgical procedures that had been done years before; operations that were adjudged necessary, but ultimately provided her with no permanent solutions to either the growth of tumor or the glaucoma in her eyes. The presence of tumor and fluid within the eyes had caused them to swell and become outsized. The left eye was nearly three times normal, its retina virtually destroyed by tumor; the right eye, less affected, was perhaps half again as large as a normal eye. The optic nerves serving both eyes had been attacked by tumor as well. The damage thus done to the precious eyes and their shape was the single worst thing that had happened to her face.

As did other plastic surgeons, Whitaker had many female patients, some of them plain women who sought to be beautiful, some of them older women who wanted to look younger. With patients such as these, Whitaker could consider the classical values he cherished, the rules that told him the nose should have just the right amount of thrust; the cheekbones height and delineation; the lips fullness; the jaw line firmness. These were the essential standards in a world that caused some women to be sexually attractive to men, other women to be ignored by them, and almost all women to be conditioned by the standard, whether they chose to acknowledge it or not.

But with Lisa, the problem was of another magnitude. She knew she could never be beautiful. She only sought to be plain enough to be left alone, to be not so different from the rest of humankind that people would recoil from the sight of her, recoil because of an unspeakable primitive fear that what had happened to her could happen to them. And so it really wasn't an aesthetic problem, at least not the kind of aesthetic problem he was used to dealing with. She did not insist upon the beauty he knew he could not provide. The medical problems within her misshapen eyes made that out of the question and it was quite clear to him that little could be done about them.

The mass of tumor had missed only the lower right side of her jaw and her chin. Whitaker carefully pressed the tumors and where they were pendulous, he lifted them up, gently, to inspect the skin underneath. He tugged a little at the good skin underneath.

"Is that uncomfortable?" he asked her. "Is anything I'm doing making you uncomfortable?"

"Only a little bit," she said softly, not looking at him, her sad face set downward, her shoulders sloping forward, her hands pressed together in her lap, the abject posture she tended to adopt when she was in public, which was frequently; neither Lisa nor her family had ever seriously considered the advantages of her not being seen by those who always hurt her. That, for them, would have been unthinkable.

"What I'm trying to see is what kind of stretch we can get out of the skin to provide coverage for the parts we take out," Whitaker continued to explain.

"If there isn't enough, will you take skin from elsewhere in the body?" she asked.

"We are thinking about that."

The rest of Lisa's body was quite clear of tumor, which is what doctors called her pathological growth of tissue. The only substantive visible evidence of the disorder were some large café-au-lait spots that were the signs, in this case, of tumors that had not developed and probably never would. The café-au-lait spots were not in themselves disfiguring and were, in fact, not much more noticeable than ordinary freckles, even though most of them were bigger than freckles.

Whitaker had large copies of pictures of Lisa's face and he drew fine lines on them, meticulously noting what he thought he would have to cut and what he thought he could leave. He placed the copies behind him, on an examination table, in such a way that Lisa could not see them, even if she had tried.

"I know you don't like to see pictures of yourself, so I'll just keep them over here." She said nothing, but nodded her appreciation and sighed softly.

It was unusual for Whitaker to be so unsure of the probable outcome, or even of precise surgical objectives, with major surgery less than two weeks away.

Precision and decisiveness had always come naturally to him. They were there when he was a boy growing up in Texas and found that he could hit a baseball well, thereby bringing to him an offer from scouts of the St. Louis Cardinals to play in their farm system, an offer he declined because he wanted to be a doctor; they were there when he decided, after medical school, that although he had a strong interest in psychiatry, it was surgery that he found most compelling—"I felt a need to see the benefits from what I was doing."

"I liked the immediate cause-effect relationships in plastic surgery, like a writer who sees graceful sentences become an article." Whitaker's love of precision was also evident to anyone

15

who took a ride of any distance with him in his brute of a BMW, during which he would invariably find some Mozart among the tapes in his glove compartment and play it, loud and clear.

As he preferred to quickly see cause and effect in the cure, so would he have liked to see it in the diagnosis. But even that was not possible. Lisa's disorder could have been inherited. But Whitaker could not determine that anyone else in her family had ever had neurofibromatosis. And so it appeared that she was a victim of it through what scientists call spontaneous mutation—a process by which there was an abnormal change in the molecular structure of one or more of the thousands of genes that gave her her individual physical and biochemical makeup. But what caused the spontaneous mutation? Nobody could say and there was no going back; Whitaker could only deal with what he saw before him.

"It is the nature of surgery," he told her, "that you see things during surgery that you didn't know before, or didn't expect entirely, and you deal with them on the spot."

"I understand."

He carefully examined her scalp and found that the evidence of the problem there was not as great as he had feared. He felt the skin on her forehead.

"It really looks quite good."

"Could it affect the scalp?" she wanted to know.

"Well, you know, it could affect any part of the body, but it hasn't affected your scalp to any significant degree," he replied, continuing an examination that was slow, tender and caring, seeming so, even in the steel and plastic and tile of the examining room. He then found what seemed to be a bony growth but thought it might not be a neurofibroma, rather something—he wasn't sure what—left from one of the eleven previous operations.

She was only twenty-one years old and she had had eleven previous surgical procedures, all of them major, all of them on her face, eyes or skull and all of them related to the neurofibromatosis.

She bore the scars and pain of these eleven procedures, but she had barely mentioned this part of her life. It would have been a dreadful enough operation to contemplate if it were going to be her first. But she had elected this and she knew what it was going to be like. She *knew*; she had been through it before. The examination continued, her occasional questions breaking softly the brittle silence of the room.

He looked at her jaw.

"Your jaw doesn't come quite as far forward as it should. There's about a quarter of an inch, six or seven millimeters up front, that we could potentially do something about, but I think we really should do first things first and deal with the more visible portions of the problem. But it's something that we could consider in the future, if you want. The surgical team involved the dental people to evaluate the jaw structure. I want to see the orthodontist's evaluation in the event that they find things that would be relatively easy to correct during surgery."

Whitaker also told her that there was some bumpiness in her lower left jaw. He thought that he could smooth it out relatively easily, through an incision he would make inside her mouth.

"I don't think that will add much to your discomfort or to the operation," he said.

"Uh-huh." She was typically noncommittal. It was impossible for anyone to say how she was taking all of this. Lisa was quite expert at keeping things to herself. At that point, I didn't fully appreciate the power of her ability to remain silent.

"It must have been frustrating to have all this surgery and see it all grow back," Whitaker said.

She nodded.

"We're hopeful," Whitaker said, his slender fingers just touching her face, "that with the more extensive removal than has been previously done, there will be less growing back, if at all, and secondly, that you're past the stage and age in your life where this thing is making much progress on your face. So those two factors, we feel, are in our favor, at least as compared to previous operations."

She nodded again and said nothing.

He thought she ought to know more about the operation itself, what would happen to her, how it would be afterward.

"You'll be able to breathe through your mouth, but not through your nose after the operation, because there will be swelling. But your nose will open up again after three or four days. You don't have any difficulty in breathing now, do you? I wouldn't expect you to have any trouble but you never know."

She shook her head and sighed. No trouble breathing. No trouble at all.

"The stitches will be left in five to seven days after surgery. I will do everything that I can possibly do to preserve the motion of your mouth," he promised.

He knew that in order to cut such large tumors out, he'd have to go deep, slicing through nerves, and he was trying, wherever possible, to avoid cutting the nerves that gave her face expression, or, at least, would give her face expression, once the tumors that had obscured all else were gone. He said he thought that saving the facial muscles around the mouth was "possible and reasonable because the neurofibromatosis is not so involved with that part of your face."

He did not offer the same prognosis for the muscles around her eyes. The tumor growth was quite extensive around her eyes.

"I really don't think we ought to try to preserve the nerve to your eyelids," he said. "I think we ought to do what's called a tarsorraphy, which is to close down the eyelids. They'll close down a little bit but they won't close the way they do now. If we do that, it's just going to compromise removal of the tumors. We'll want to trim your eyebrows down . . ."

"That's fine with me."

". . . and then we'll take out skin from around both eyes, more on the left than on the right, so that means incisions. But you already have scars there, it's not going to be very different in terms of the amount of scars that you see there."

"Scars don't bother me," Lisa said.

"Then we'll make direct excisions, again scars, but we'll try to use the natural folds between the nose and the mouth. We'll also thin your nose down quite a lot, so we can give you a little more projection of your nose by taking the cartilage from one of the ribs and give your nose a little more shape."

Lisa heard it all and nodded quietly. She just said, "I understand," and had no questions.

There was a good chance that she would lose her ability to blink and perhaps even to smile in all of this and *she had no questions*. It was a price she was more than willing to pay. She had already decided that, and for her it had not been such a difficult decision to make.

As Whitaker looked at her under the white light, it occurred to him, as it had before, that this really was not such a bad face. It might have sounded curious, perhaps unbelievable to her if he had told her then, but it was the way he had always felt about her.

Despite the deformity, Lisa's face, to Whitaker, had a certain appeal. He could not have said easily what there might be about such a face that he liked, but undeniably, there was something. And he was able to see it, honestly, because unlike most of the other strangers who had come into Lisa's life, he had quickly gotten beyond her face. He had worked to improve many faces, twisted and troubled, and so he had learned to move beyond them. Her face did not disturb his sensibilities, his traditional and strongly held values on feminine beauty.

He told me that for him, something good had managed to assert itself on that face, amid all the tumor, something that came from deep within her and bespoke her patience, her sadness, her ability to endure extraordinary abuse from strangers. Perhaps all of this said more about Whitaker than it did about Lisa, because as much as faces fascinated him, he was always quick to say that no conclusions could be drawn from them

19

about the characters of their owners. Lisa knew there were people like Whitaker, whose compassion and intellect could penetrate a face, or ignore it. But there were not enough of them. And there was no going back. Not for her. If she made it through this examination, she would have a new face, a face she had to have.

"And there is this bony irregularity," Whitaker continued, peering at the left side of her head. "There is a bony problem in addition to the soft tissue problem. I think it's extremely likely that we'll want to replace this bone with another bone, which means we'll take a bone from your rib and transplant it up there. It is done through a two-inch incision. As I tell everyone, it isn't a source for concern, because the bones taken from your ribs grow back. At less than thirty-five years of age, you can expect it to grow back. That's a real plus. You're really not losing anything."

Whitaker's plans for Lisa's face, though tentative, were radical, more radical than anything he had ever read about in professional journals. Her face, of necessity, was thus undergoing something of a metamorphosis in his mind's eye, becoming a surgical target, becoming the physical abstraction all surgeons must see if they are to operate effectively, decisively, accurately, impersonally. The impersonal abstraction must be there even if the surgeon is working on the face, that most unabstract and personal expression of the individual. It was serious to contemplate and he had nobody to ask for guidelines. He knew he could consider such a surgery only because so many other surgeons had tried before him, not only on Lisa, but on other people with other kinds of afflictions. Fine surgeons had tried less radical surgery for neurofibromatosis, which always seemed to grow back, sometimes slowly, sometimes quickly, always implacably. They could not be faulted. Whitaker knew that. They had been as bold as they dared, as bold as their wisdom and skills permitted, as bold as their patients had courage. But this would be his operation. His responsibility. His triumph or his failure. And yet it occurred to him, even as he prepared to give a young woman a new face, the old face was not such a bad face.

As this face became his target, he thought of other faces, other targets, those of his colleagues. It was the most severe case of neurofibromatosis to the face that he had ever seen. There had been no face like this, no face that he knew of where the tumor had claimed and conquered so much. He had seen other severe cases of neurofibromatosis, but usually only a portion of the face was involved, sometimes as much as half. In this face, both hemispheres were involved. When other victims were lucky, and that seemed to be a reasonable percentage of the time, their faces simply had a craggy or bumpy look, a look that seemed far more appropriate in men than in women.

Lisa's face. Even after days when he had had long and arduous surgical procedures, Whitaker would think of it and what he might do to change, improve, remake.

But it was hardly like a sculptor looking at a piece of Carrara. There was enormous danger. There is always some danger in surgery but with Lisa, Whitaker had added concerns. Lisa's surgery looked as if it would be especially bloody. The tumors were massive, vascular, and Whitaker knew there really was no way to avoid extensive bleeding once they were cut. But he stared at Lisa's face, trying to determine how he might avoid the unavoidable, or at least minimize it, trying to anticipate things that could not be anticipated.

"Why," he asked her, "must you be such a challenge?"

Chapter Three

Whitaker continued his examination of Lisa's face, studying the tumors he planned to remove, drawing lines on the picture of Lisa's face.

Across the room, toward the door, there was a woman daydreaming. Her name was Verna Mitros. She was leaning against the doorframe to Examination Room No. 9, away from the white light, her hands jammed into the pockets of her raincoat, staring at the examination, yet not really seeing any of it.

It was she who had brought Lisa for this examination; brought Lisa to all of her visits with Whitaker. Indeed, Verna had brought Lisa to Whitaker's attention in the first place.

The examination had started quietly enough and the routine nature of some of the early questions had permitted Verna to drift into her reverie. But then Whitaker had told Lisa that there would be scars, that she might not be able to blink, might not be able to smile, ever again, might never be able to show any expression. Verna had heard it. Lisa had accepted it. Now Whitaker's words began to burr into the daydream. The present became insistent, uncomfortable, intolerable.

"I wanted to talk to you about that left eye of yours," he said to Lisa. Lisa's head drooped even lower. "You haven't seen Dr. Katowitz recently, have you?"

"I'm going to see him this afternoon."

"Well," Whitaker said, his voice softer, "he's going to talk to you about removing that left eye."

"Do you *have* to do it?"

"No, we don't have to do it. If you really feel as though you'd like to keep that eye, we can certainly do that. But we both feel that it would improve the chances for cure . . . sorry. We're not going to *cure* the problem. It will improve the chances of getting as much [of the tumor] out as possible and having a more long-lasting effect. Plus, it will improve your appearance. I think you ought to talk to him about it and I leave the rest of it to you and to him. Whatever you decide is what we will do."

"Do you have to know right away?" Her small voice seemed to quaver slightly for the first time.

"No. You don't have to make that decision now. You can leave the decision and we can leave the eye. We're trying to make this the big operation and do as much as we can at this time. I am certain there will be more operations. We'd like those to be relatively minor. I just think that, psychologically, it's better for you to have one big event, and after that just minor revisions. But if you want to take care of the eye later, that's fine. It's certainly up to you."

Verna stared at the two of them in the circle of light. Now they were in sharp focus.

"We talked about risk the first time you came in," Whitaker continued. "It is important for us to state there is risk. It is a big operation. It has every risk conceivable, including the ultimate risk of not surviving the operation. I think that not surviving is extraordinarily unlikely. We never had anybody not survive an operation. But it is something that we all have to be aware of and we will take every precaution. The main thing that concerns us is that these are very vascular tumors and they're going to bleed a lot. We'll do everything possible to cut down on the bleeding. Sometimes we even have to stop operations in the middle if the bleeding looks like it will threaten a life. If it looked like it were threatening your life, I would certainly stop it."

Whitaker paused again and then he said, "I want you to understand that as clearly as possible. The first concern, as far as I am concerned, is having you alive and healthy. My second concern is trying to improve the condition of your face. Are you with me on this?"

"I'm not worried, Dr. Whitaker. I know it will be all right."

"I'll wait outside," Verna blurted out quickly, startling the two of them.

"Are you all right?" Whitaker asked. "Is everything all right?"

"I'll wait outside," Verna said, her voice flat. She opened the door quickly and left without another word. She was nauseous, her heart was pounding, the walls of the hallway closed in on her. She stood outside the room in the hallway and she was sure she was going to become very ill.

She suffered the ultimate penalty familiar to those who have ever tried to help someone else in a serious way. And so she thought about herself as helper-become-meddler: *An eye. He said he might have to remove an eye. And in the bargain, Lisa might be lost. Her mother would rather have her the way she is than dead. Part of this will have to be on me. It will be my fault, my fault. It never occurred to me that she could lose her life. What have I done?* She fought to compose herself. *I have to drive Lisa home. I can't let her see me like this.*

On the way home that night, she was silent. Lisa asked her if she were all right.

"Oh, I'm fine. The air was a little close in that room, that's all."

Lisa hadn't noticed that the air was close. The trip home was uneventful.

It was the second time that Verna had decided to battle with neurofibromatosis. Victory had eluded her and her reward for her valor was guilt. She knew her guilt was irrational, but she suffered from it anyhow. The guilt had set in after she lost the first battle in 1979. That was long before she had met or heard of Lisa. It had started because of her concern for her friend, Margaret.

Margaret was a special friend of long standing and a victim of neurofibromatosis. Verna had always empathized, but really didn't know what it was all about, except that Margaret's body was covered with small but ugly tumors, thousands of them, it seemed, from the neck down; thousands of tumors hidden under turtleneck sweaters and high-neck blouses of sturdy material that she invariably wore. There were tumors on her face, too, but they were the tiniest of bumps, barely visible, easily hidden and minimized under makeup, and so Margaret looked quite presentable to the world around her. In the sense that she evaded instant rejection and acts of vicious abuse and aggression in public places, her situation was just the reverse of Lisa's. But life was not really all that pleasant for Margaret. She knew a different kind of razor-sharp shunning; she had been ultimately rejected by every man she had ever known.

For Verna, who had a satisfying life, Margaret's straits were impossible to forget or to put aside. She therefore took it upon herself to write to the National Institutes of Health in Bethesda, Md., asking about a cure, because she refused to permit herself to believe that there was no cure. And after she learned it, she refused to accept it.

Somebody in Washington referred her to the National Neurofibromatosis Foundation, only recently founded, with headquarters at 70 West 40th Street in New York City. Verna brought Margaret and Margaret's mother up to New York and met Dr. Allan E. Rubenstein, chairman of the foundation's Medical Advisory Board and a member of the staff at the Mount Sinai Hospital. Rubenstein was then one of the relatively few physicians in the United States engaged in basic research on neurofibromatosis, one of the few trying to understand its growth in the autonomic nervous system, the system that controls the heart muscle, the respiratory system and the skin.

He essentially repeated what the people in Washington had said: there was no cure, no treatment other than the surgical removal of tumors. He noted that in some victims, the tumors seemed to grow very slowly after puberty. For them, surgical removal of the growths might provide some relief for many years.

Rubenstein's personal interest was in determining if there might be a biochemical way to alter and thus correct the message that an individual's genetic code sent to the cells to preclude or stop tumor growth. That, in his opinion, would constitute a "cure."

Margaret heard him out. Given the nature of her case, she concluded that surgery was out of the question.

Surgery or no surgery, Margaret decided she should at the very least become familiar with whatever advances research might make in the years to come. She joined a Philadelphia area chapter of the National Neurofibromatosis Foundation. Verna joined with her. The members of the chapter, some of them victims of the disorder, others the parents of children who had it, agreed to meet on Tuesdays. Verna suggested that their next meeting—only the second one in their brief existence—be held at her home.

At that point, she was already a member of a parapsychology group that had been meeting for a couple of years. It was established by another friend and purported to deal with everything from psychokinesis to extrasensory perception to clairvoyance to the spectrum of human thought that surrounds but is outside the realm of orthodox psychology. Verna described the group as just friends who were looking for answers "talking on every single subject possible, on self-healing, on keeping a balance within yourself . . . sort of a self-help group."

The parapsychologists met every Friday night at Verna's house in Belmont Hills, which is at the back door of Philadelphia's Main Line. The members, relaxed but ready to be vocal, reflective, fanciful, assertive, even combative, would file in and casually arrange themselves in chairs or, more frequently, on the thick black carpeting that covered the large living room. They liked to sit around a large handsome cocktail table made of glass, wood and brass, there to talk about, and attempt to find answers to, some of the problems people have wondered about over the millennia.

On the Friday before the Tuesday that the neurofibromatosis group was to visit the same living room, Verna decided she wanted to tell the parapsychologists about Margaret and neurofibromatosis. Margaret was not a parapsychologist and Verna had a need to talk about an affliction that was awesome, unfair, outrageous, so beyond her control. In four days, the room would be filled with people who had to deal with it directly.

At first, Verna had no intention of saying anything about it. But as she sat there, listening to the parapsychologists describe their wonderment, their perceptions, their problems, her frustrations at being unable to solve Margaret's problem came to the fore. The precise triggering device was a comment made by one member of the group, who was an epileptic. He had had an accident at work, was out on disability, was having a dispute with the company he worked for, and wanted to talk about it.

"My life's a mess," he said. "There's never enough money, the kids seem to need more and more and I can't work, I can't . . ."

Verna tore into him.

"You think you have it bad? You have your sight, you're handsome, you're basically a healthy guy. Okay, so you have to do without a lot of things, but they are not the most important things of life. You don't know what real trouble is. You should see some of the people I have seen, people who have *real* problems. Then you'd know."

She knew most of the people in her parapsychology group had never heard of neurofibromatosis and had a lot of misconceptions about what the Elephant Man's Disease was all about. Maybe they ought to know, she thought, as she lectured the surprised epileptic. That would help them put their lives into perspective. They ought to know.

A woman named Vera Lukens, seated at Verna's right, heard

the description of Margaret's problem and how impossible it all seemed.

"I also know someone who has it," she said.

"*You* do?" Verna was a little surprised to find someone else who knew about neurofibromatosis. Margaret had seemed so isolated to her, so lonely because so many people did not understand.

"Yes," Vera Lukens said. "Her name is Lisa. Her mother is an old friend of mine and her family has just about given up hope of ever finding a solution in her case."

"You have her mother get in touch with me tomorrow," Verna told her, "because the local NF group is meeting here on Tuesday night. I'd like Lisa and her mother to come. I promise you, we'll get help for her."

All of this may have seemed a little odd, even to the feisty and free-wheeling parapsychologists. Here Verna had essentially just told an epileptic that he didn't really know what hopelessness was and now she was soliciting a telephone call from the mother of a young woman who had severe and incurable neurofibromatosis. Verna appeared to be holding out hope where, it seemed to them, there was none. But they also knew that Verna was easily as stubborn as she was compassionate.

Vera called Mary and Mary called Verna the next day. They spoke on the telephone for an hour and a half. Mary told Verna that she had tried to find someone, anyone, who would be able to help her daughter. She had even asked the customers at every restaurant she ever worked for, since Lisa's birth, twenty-one years before. It did not matter who the customers were or if they knew anything about medicine. Mary asked them anyhow.

"I figure it never hurts to try," Mary said. "You never know. There was always a chance that someone would come in and order a meal and know all about whatever this is."

Mary wept several times during that conversation. She was an optimistic woman by nature. But whenever she was asked about the past, about the years and the abuse that she had shared with Lisa, tears invariably welled up in her eyes. That night, on the telephone, was such an occasion.

Her customers had wanted to help her, she said, but there was nothing that they or anyone else could do for her daughter. Mary knew there wasn't any medicine that would work and she was convinced that more operations would be futile. Lisa had had many operations, and the tumors only grew back.

Even so, Lisa's life had not been a waste, Mary said. She told Verna how proud she was that Lisa had once been invited to be a flower girl at a wedding, and that she had done it well, as she had done so many things that people with normal faces take for granted. Mary had seen to it that her daughter did such things with excellence.

"I always told her," Mary said, "that she was as good as the next person. That's because she is." All she wanted was to do normal things with people outside the family. But for the most part, it had not been possible.

"I know there's help for Lisa, I just know it," Verna said, explaining her interest in the neurofibromatosis group that would soon visit her home. "Will you come to a meeting that we're going to have at my house next Tuesday?"

"We'll both be there," Mary promised.

As Rubenstein had told her, Verna knew there was no cure. But that did not mean there was no help.

The Tuesday meeting was orderly, uneventful, attended by fourteen people, including Mary and Lisa. There was one interesting contrast with the parapsychology group. Whereas many of the parapsychologists had arranged themselves on the carpet, the members of the neurofibromatosis group all took chairs. It had nothing to do with any physical damage the disorder might have done to any of them. But somehow, when people considered a problem as frightening as neurofibromatosis, they wanted to be seated formally. The vulnerability that came with the comfort of lounging seemed inappropriate when such tragedies were discussed. Lisa said nothing. She had not even wanted to be present at the meeting; she was uneasy with such a group. She had always preferred to handle her problems alone, or with the help of her family. Discussing something of this sort outside the family was uncomfortable for her.

Mary, naturally gregarious, ever trusting of strangers, had no such reservations. She had already talked of Lisa to most of the steady customers where she was a waitress. It would have been unseemly not to talk to these people.

She told them how long she had been trying to find help and they listened to her sympathetically enough. But they could not tell her there was a cure, because there was none.

Verna telephoned Rubenstein in New York the next morning to tell him all about Lisa. She had not spoken to him since visiting him with Margaret, more than a year before. Rubenstein told her that the situation he had described to her had not really changed.

Nevertheless, he suggested she bring Lisa to New York, where, he said, he knew a good plastic surgeon who might be able to remove the growths.

Verna declined his invitation to bring Lisa to New York.

"It won't work," she told him. "That would involve a lot of trips over a long period of time. Her family would want to stay with her and they certainly can't afford anything like that."

Verna was insistent that Rubenstein help her find someone in Philadelphia, and Rubenstein would later remember her as "a very aggressive woman who seems to be eager to get people taken care of."

He then referred her to Dr. Anna Meadows, a pediatric oncologist who headed the neurofibromatosis clinic at Children's Hospital, which is part of the University of Pennsylvania's medical complex centered on 34th and Spruce. Meadows was away when Verna called, but Dr. Angela Obringer, an associate of Meadows, was there in her stead and referred Verna to Whitaker.

Verna called Whitaker's office, and as she started to talk to Elaine Stevens, Whitaker's secretary, it occurred to her that she was going too far. Lisa knew nothing about this. Nor did Mary. It was a call that Lisa herself ought to be making, if indeed Lisa were interested. And so Verna cut the conversation short, telling Elaine Stevens why.

Not long after, Lisa called Miss Stevens and the amiable young secretary would remember it well:

"This soft little voice was on the end of the phone . . . just very, very soft . . . and I was having a hard time trying to understand what she was saying. Then I realized that she was crying, sobbing. She was trying to explain to me what her problem was. She said that she had heard about Dr. Whitaker and that she wanted a chance to see him. All she wanted was a chance to see if he could do anything for her."

Miss Stevens scheduled the appointment for 11:45 on the morning of April 28, 1981. That was a Tuesday. Verna figured she'd take the day off from her job at Robinson Associates, a market research firm in Bryn Mawr. There she held the title of internal coordinator, which essentially meant that she was office manager.

She went directly to Michael DeVita, then Robinson's vice-president in charge of data processing. She anticipated his cooperation; she was not disappointed.

"Sure, take as much time as you like," DeVita said. "Most people wouldn't bother." DeVita knew that even if she tried, Verna couldn't take all the compensatory time she had coming.

She checked in at her office that morning, but left long before she had to. Before 11 o'clock, her aging but low-mileage Dodge poked its nose into the dead-end street where Lisa lived, Prospect Terrace.

By any reasonable American standard, it was a nice neighborhood to watch springs come and go, Verna could see that. At least it was for ordinary young people with ordinary young friends. Lisa's house was a small one in the middle of the block. Behind it, just beyond Verna's line of vision, were several species of washers, dryers and gasoline-powered mowers, harvested from neighbors by Lisa's father, Harry, who knew they'd be after him soon if he hadn't finished all of the repairs they wanted. Closer to the cellar were little pieces of engine parts and aluminum and cast-offs from one place or another. Harry was regarded in the neighborhood as a clever man in repairing things, a handy person who could fix anything. But it was in spring, when homeowners waited for their mowers to be fixed, that he was probably most appreciated.

Verna was prompt—she was always prompt—and off they went, through Lisa's hometown. They went by bars with fronts made of artificial stone, houses with aluminum awnings hanging over new bricks, past carry-outs and eat-ins and a great many service stations, slowly descending all the way to the Schuylkill Expressway, leading to Philadelphia. Lisa slouched down in the front seat next to Verna, not saying very much to Verna's cheerful chatter on a pleasant spring day.

Lisa had called Elaine Stevens crying, not crying for joy because she had found someone who could help her, but crying from frustration, because she doubted that anyone could help her. She did not look forward to meeting with this surgeon named Whitaker. She was feeling defensive, irritable, grateful for Verna's interest and kindness, but almost resenting that she had agreed to do anything at all. There had been too many disappointments, too many broken promises, too many doctors who had poked and looked and sighed and finally said they could do nothing.

They arrived a bit early and parked their car a few blocks from the Hospital of the University of Pennsylvania, because they weren't sure there was parking there (there was). They walked to the hospital's Silverstein Pavilion, through its busy lobby, and took the elevator up to the fourth floor, where they entered a large waiting room carpeted in beige tweed. At one end of it there were nurses who assisted physicians in their examinations and next to them, nearest the door, were the receptionists. The room was crowded at that hour and Gloria Iannone, one of the receptionists, handled the paperwork.

Miss Iannone typed out one of the short blue forms, asking

Lisa her name, age, date of birth, telephone number, billing address, her living address, her next of kin, referring physician and Blue Shield number. Each question was followed by the rapid-fire soft thud of Miss Iannone's electric typewriter and Lisa's voice was so soft that Miss Iannone had trouble, at times, hearing her answers. Miss Iannone then notified Miss Stevens that Lisa was there, but Whitaker was late and so Lisa and Verna sat there in deep leather-like chairs, both of them looking at, but not really seeing, a couple of paintings of flowers on two walls and a hunt-chase scene on another wall. There were other patients there interested in investigating plastic surgery possibilities for themselves. From time to time, some of them would stare at Lisa. They had problems with their faces, or thought they did. But they were thankful that they did not have Lisa's problem. Thankful and fearful, just like everybody else.

Verna and Lisa sat and waited, Lisa staring at the tweed carpet, saying almost nothing to Verna. Verna did not try to induce her to talk; it was quite enough that Lisa had come this far. At this point, it had been ten years since Lisa's last plastic surgery and she had vowed many times that she would never do it again. She was rather astonished that she had actually agreed to all of this and found herself sitting there, waiting to see a man she did not really want to see.

Miss Stevens knew that Whitaker was running behind; he had a heavy surgery schedule that day and even if he hadn't, he was escorting a fellow surgeon, Dr. Oscar Contreras of Santiago, Chile, who was spending a few days at the hospital, just observing, as visiting surgeons are wont to do.

Quite soon, though, Lisa was asked to go into Examining Room No. 9, which is at the far end of the corridor leading to Whitaker's office.

The first professional to see her was Dr. Eric Blomain. He had taken a six-month sabbatical from his duties at the Hershey Medical Center, Pennsylvania State University, to work as a fellow with Whitaker, so that he could learn more about craniofacial surgery. He functioned, as did all Whitaker's fellows, as an aide-de-camp and troubleshooter. Blomain would never forget the meeting, even though he saw hundreds of patients after he saw Lisa:

"When I walked in, she seemed ill at ease, leaning against the examination bed, looking anxious. I had been told she had neurofibromatosis but I did not expect it to this degree. I studied her face, making the rough notes I'd give to Dr. Whitaker.

"I apologize for seeming to stare at you," he told her, "but I have to in order to do my job." Lisa very much appreciated Blomain's having the sensitivity and courtesy to say that, but at the time, she showed him no appreciation—only hostility and suspicion.

"Do you think you can really help me or is this a waste of time?" she asked him.

"I think we can help you if you have a lot of patience. And it depends on your endurance and our endurance."

"Do you really think so?" she began to sob. "Can you really help me?"

"I think that Dr. Whitaker might be able to do it," Blomain said.

Whitaker returned to his office with Contreras and Blomain delivered his report, which was not overly hopeful, while Lisa waited in the examining room. Minutes later, Lisa met Whitaker for the first time.

Lisa's initial impression of Whitaker was not a good one. To her, he seemed distant, preoccupied, weary. She had seen that sort of aloofness in other surgeons. She was not impressed with it. Surgeons were frequently lofty, icy, but all that loftiness and presumed cosmic knowledge had not helped her. But if Whitaker seemed distant, he also seemed interested, confident. Perhaps, she thought, he was even competent. That would be nice. She would proceed with Whitaker, she thought. She had no commitment. She could always stop going to him if she thought that he was suggesting something pointless.

Lisa had quite a number of meetings with Whitaker in the months that followed. Each time, Whitaker somehow seemed less aloof to her, and a friendship started to develop between them, but Lisa firmly controlled her optimism as well as her need for new friends. Nothing had worked before. Why should this?

Over the weeks and months that followed, Verna relinquished vacation days and days owed her as compensatory time and took Lisa to all the appointments. Mary could not have done it. She was working as a waitress. Lisa's sisters could have done it only with great difficulty. And Verna wanted to do it.

These were good times for both of them, especially for Lisa. She once gave Verna a box of candy; another time a potted plant. Mary believes, and Lisa agrees, that when somebody does something for you, you have to say more than thank you. You never take anything for granted.

One mild spring day it was raining hard when they emerged from Whitaker's office and Verna's car was parked at the other end of the University of Pennsylvania campus.

They took off their shoes and in their stocking feet ran together through the rain, laughing over puddles that lie in Penn's red brick roadlets, bounding around groups of students huddled under umbrellas, students trying to keep their books dry under plastic ponchos.

"I suppose everybody thinks we're crazy," Lisa said.

"What do we care? We *are* crazy," Verna answered.

They were both drenched that day by the time they reached the reliable Dodge, which then promptly and unreliably overheated in rush-hour traffic.

"It's really a neat car," Verna insists, "with only 40,000 miles on it. It had never done that before. But I knew it would blow up if I didn't get it off the road and shut it off." They had a mediocre dinner but a good time in Philadelphia that evening, just talking. It is a day they both remember.

Another day they remember is when Whitaker asked Lisa to have her picture taken and Verna took her to the photographer's studio, which was on campus, some distance from Whitaker's office. Verna recalls it this way:

"We came out of the photographer's office, and I said, 'Hey, let's go out this door.' Even though there was a sign that said 'DO NOT USE THIS DOOR' or something like that. And O.K., we went out that door and the siren went off. I grabbed Lisa's hand and we ran along a corridor, going toward the library, I think. Someone came running toward us, laughing. I told him, 'I didn't do it, *she did it*.' Lisa was just roaring the whole time; we were the funniest people you'd ever seen, two idiots running through the library, laughing, with the siren going, so much noise. I suppose it doesn't sound like much in the telling, but at the time it was, and we had such a good time together."

One time in the car going home after a visit to Whitaker, Verna said to Lisa, "You've gotten a lot of attention in your life, negative maybe, but a lot of attention, with people looking at you all the time. I wonder if you're going to miss that if and when the time comes that you're normal."

"I don't know," Lisa said.

"Of course you don't. It can't be answered at this end of it, it's got to be answered at the other end, *when you walk through a crowd and nobody turns to look at you*."

There was a day when Lisa asked Verna if she thought it was all going to work.

"You know what I think?"

"What?"

"I think that after this is all over, you're only going to have one major decision to make."

"What's that?"

"Whether or not to take the pill."

They laughed together as they drove home in Verna's reliable car.

As for Whitaker, he was struck with how well-adjusted Lisa seemed to be. But he wanted to make sure that she was strong enough emotionally to deal with what might be ahead. He asked her to see a psychiatrist at Penn, Dr. Michael Pertschuk, who, among other things, asked Lisa what her long-range plans for the future were.

"Doctor, I don't make long-range plans for the future," she said.

36

Chapter Four

Lisa had to have come from somewhere. She had to have been nurtured in a very special way; all of that determination had to spring from most extraordinary circumstances.

She was preparing to do something that many other people might not have done under the same circumstances. Others might have felt the risk was too high and that solitude was not that bad.

I suggested that once to Lisa and she replied, "You can't say that. You haven't been there."

It could have been argued that her problem was more severe because she was a woman. Lisa, although a 21-year-old in the 1980s, made it clear that she had many of the values women seemed to cherish, more openly and without question at least, in the 1950s: a husband, a home, children, a conventional, traditional American way of life. She was thus heir to a somewhat tattered, disparaged dream, one that glorified young women and ignored older ones.

But Lisa never had been given the first part of the dream. All she had ever known was the cruelest, most brutal kind of shunning. And so it seemed as if her hurt might be of a larger magnitude than it would have been had she been a man; men are never put on that kind of pedestal. But then there was Merrick, the Elephant Man, and what happened to him. With beings such as Lisa and Merrick, the penalties are sadly the same.

As the penalties were the same, so, it seemed, were there similarities in the armor developed by both Merrick and Lisa to deal with whatever life had to offer. Merrick, like Lisa, was born to a working-class family. Moreover, it seemed that what Frederick Treves wrote about his famous patient might also be said of Lisa. Like Merrick, she had "passed through the fire and had come out unscathed." Like Merrick, she had taken much abuse and, if one might borrow a description from Treves, she was neither a "spiteful, malignant misanthrope, swollen with venom," nor was she "a despairing melancholic on the verge of idiocy." And the reasons seemed to lie in the most striking similarity of all: the love they received from their mothers. From what we know of Merrick, his mother was the only person who really cared about him until he entered London Hospital. Lisa also received the care of a mother capable of great love, an intelligent, patient, giving mother. Moreover, Mary's love was powerfully reinforced by three older sisters who spent much time with Lisa. Merrick had had no such advantage.

With all the similarities, there was a major difference between the two, aside from their sex and the eras into which they were born: Merrick had no real hope that surgery could cure his deformity. The record of his life from Treves and Montagu suggests that although he may have never abandoned his desire to look like others, he nevertheless made peace with his lot and lived his life as well as anyone could under such circumstances. He once told Treves, after the hospital had taken him in and tended to his needs, "I am happy every hour of the day." Treves referred to him as "one of the most contented creatures I have chanced to meet."

Lisa, although keeping her perspective and even her wry sense of humor intact throughout her childhood, never expressed to me, in our many hours of conversations, the level of happiness that Merrick seems to have enjoyed when he was secure in London Hospital.

"I could have handled the way I look if they could have handled it," she said of her critics and their standards. "I know the way things are and I know the way they should be and they are not the way they should be."

Lisa, in contrast to Merrick, had been conditioned over many years to keep the hope for a cure alive. There was a part of her that always believed that someone, something would come along that would deliver her into the world of physical normality. Her outlook reflected her mother's optimism. It was more than just being part of an age of scientific wonder, where so many problems are solved or seem susceptible to solution.

Mary H. was surprisingly willing to talk about the bleak past, not to trumpet all that she had tried to do for her daughter, but to recount, with great care, what had happened before and during her final pregnancy, the pregnancy that gave her Lisa.

It was a most uncommon pregnancy. There had been no waves of nausea in the morning, no undue swelling of her breasts, no change of pigmentation around the nipples, no prescient feeling of life within her body, as she had sensed it and seen it in four previous pregnancies. Mary's fifth and final pregnancy was a pregnancy unplanned, unexpected, not even formally confirmed by her physician until after three months had passed.

Menstruation had ceased, as it should have, the first month after conception had taken place. One month went by and then another. But Mary was already forty-four years old and she mistakenly presumed that she might be in the initial stages of menopause, which can begin much earlier than the age of forty-four.

"I really didn't think I could become pregnant. At my age, you just don't think about things like that; pregnancy was the last thing in my mind," she told me. "At my age, who wanted to have a baby? They tell you that you can never be sure, but I didn't even dream it was possible."

She did not go to a physician sooner because the family income, derived mostly from her wages as a waitress, permitted essentials, not much more.

But by the end of the third month, Mary was able to feel a soft lump above the pubic bone and so when she asked her doctor to do a "rabbit" test, it was only something of a formality. She knew, although she would not admit it, even to herself. She loved all her children dearly, and everybody else's children, too, it frequently seemed to her neighbors. But raising her children and working full time, cleaning homes for the well-to-do and waiting on tables for all those years, had been difficult, almost unbearable at times.

Now that her youngest, Diane, was fifteen years old, Mary thought that the responsibilities of parenthood would soon be put behind her. She had wanted that, wanted it desperately. She loved them but she was relieved that they were growing up and that she was still young enough to enjoy life. Contrary to the teachings of her Roman Catholic faith, she had used contraceptive devices in what appeared to be an only partially successful effort to control the size of her family.

"Yes, I used contraceptives, but it seemed like I got pregnant anyhow. I originally thought I was one of the lucky ones. No matter what I used, I got pregnant."

The proof was her eldest daughter, Arlene, who had been created despite the fact that conception had occurred during a time when contraception was always used.

But that unplanned birth had not caused consternation; Mary wanted to have more children eventually. The defiance of her own fecundity to modern birth-control measures was, however, unsettling as well as amusing. It was even a little gratifying; the power to create life is hardly a trifle, even to a woman who can do it easily.

The final pregnancy was a much more serious thing to contemplate. Mary still loved babies and seemed to have both limitless patience and extraordinary skill in bringing out the best in them, but she felt there was a time when parenting should be and could be properly put aside.

When the rabbit test was scheduled, Mary asked Arlene, then twenty-three years old, to drive her to a laboratory in Norristown recommended to her by her doctor. Arlene was more than a little alarmed; her mother seemed always well, always sturdy, vital, the antithesis of the fragile female of the 1950s. She knew that Mary would not be going to a clinic unless there were a good reason.

"What's this all about?" she demanded of her mother.

"It's just a little something that I want to find out about," Mary reassured her. "I think it's just a mild kidney infection."

When the laboratory reported its results to her physician, Mary drove the car herself to hear the physician recite the scientific findings that she already knew empirically. There was no point in involving Arlene. Or anyone else.

"I broke down and cried when the doctor told me. I was having a hard enough time raising four. In fact, I was so upset that I couldn't tell the kids. I told Harry right away and he really didn't say much of anything. He sort of shrugged it off and said, 'Well, if that's the way it is, that's it,' and he was the one who told the kids."

Arlene does not remember their father actually telling them anything, at least not as a group. Jennifer, a middle daughter, does recall that her father informed her that a baby was on the way. In any event, the daughters knew about the pregnancy quickly, however slow Harry seemed to move to inform them. Tom, Mary and Harry's only son, was the last to know; by that time, he had married and moved some distance away. When Jennifer heard, she said she thought it might be nice to have a baby in the house after all these years. At least, that is what she told her disconsolate mother. Arlene and Diane were less enthusiastic. Jennifer was eighteen years old and she was expected to leave the house soon to work, marry, and establish her own household. She wasn't engaged yet, but nobody believed that attractive, vivacious Jennifer would remain single for long. And so it figured that the disruptions caused by a new baby would be most felt by Arlene, who, since her husband was away in the

Air Force, lived in a small frame house conveniently behind the one occupied by her parents and sisters; and by Diane, who was still in high school. Arlene and Diane were by no means hostile to the pregnancy. But they teased Jennifer that she would share fully in the fun of the baby, but less than fully in the drudgery that would invariably accompany the fun.

Mary regarded the advent of new birth with resignation. She was neither sad nor joyous. She would do her duty. She gave no thought to abortion. Even if one could have been done properly and legally, Mary's personal sensibilities, and her strongly held Roman Catholicism, would have precluded it. She did believe in the "rhythm" method of family planning, which was in accordance with Church teachings, and as so many other Catholics apparently do these days, she also used artificial means of preventing conception, which was decidedly not in accordance with any policy enunciated by Rome. In any event, neither approach could be trusted to work. Mary never became a member or supporter of the Right-to-Life movement and always tended to feel that such decisions are best made by individuals. It was just that for her, an abortion would have been out of the question, far more unacceptable than the hard work that promised to attend new life. For her, pregnancy meant a child, and a child had to be born and raised. There was no other way; it was the order of things. No matter that a woman no longer young might be weary, might feel the need for more freedom and less responsibility, might not be quite so able to give and forgive and understand and sacrifice constantly, as she had already done and as good mothers are supposed to do.

It might have been different if she felt that the pregnancy involved a clear-cut threat to her life or to the health of the baby. But at the beginning of the pregnancy, there was no hint of that. A late pregnancy did not necessarily mean a difficult one. There was no risk that was obvious to the mother. There was no suggestion in her mind that this child would somehow be less loved than the others. And there was no hint that the fetus growing within Mary would be the victim of one of the strangest and cruelest of the many genetic abominations known to science. In short, there really was no alternative for Mary H.; the pregnancy would go to term.

She was mindful that twenty-six years had elapsed since her first pregnancy, which had occurred before her nineteenth birthday, when, like all teenagers, she could not believe she would ever have less than boundless energy, let alone become middle-aged. Fifteen years had gone by since her fourth pregnancy, which had given her Diane and which she had mistakenly thought would be her last. It had been so long that Mary had to refresh herself about details of the regimen that all caring, expectant mothers must follow and she wearily but dutifully began to think, once again, about nutrition, about drinking milk, about seeing to it that she did not gain too much weight. There wasn't much joy in it for her. But she did what she knew she had to do. Mary had always done what she had to do.

Her feelings were nothing like those she had in 1934, when Tom was born. It had been an easy first pregnancy for the robust daughter of Ukrainian immigrants, herself one of eight children. And it was a welcome pregnancy, Great Depression or not.

"I did the polka the night before he was born. My brother-in-law had a tap room and we were having a wonderful time dancing when the labor pains started. I walked into the hospital and they said to me, 'What are *you* doing here?' And I told them I was having labor pains and it was time but they looked at me and said, 'Maybe you ought to come back in a couple of months.' No, no, I'm ready, I told them. Look up your own records. They did, and admitted me immediately, and Tommy was born the next day. I guess I knew from the beginning that I was pregnant with Tommy. After the first month, anyhow. Sometimes you know right away. Other times you don't."

Through all of her pregnancies, Mary had worked for as long as she could: as a depression-era cleaning woman who earned three dollars a week; as a punch-press operator in a factory in

Philadelphia that made farm tools and children's sleds; and as a waitress at a country club and in several other locations in southeastern Pennsylvania. At one point during the depression, she did housework from seven o'clock in the morning until six o'clock at night, with a half-day on Saturday. Her take-home pay averaged five dollars a week. It frequently proved not enough to put food on the table.

"When I cleaned house, I counted on getting something to eat, too. There was one job I did and she never gave me anything to eat. I worked all day and then I'd come home crying and there was nothing to eat there, either. My mother asked me why they didn't and I told her those people went out to eat. It didn't occur to them to put something in the refrigerator, since they never looked in there themselves."

Mary learned that to be in contact with the rich did not necessarily mean that she would derive rich benefits.

"Once, when I was a waitress at the country club, we had a party of eighteen people for New Year's Eve. Doctors and lawyers, all of them. I was assigned to their table all night. I served them their dinner, I served them drinks, I served them breakfast, and when they left, you know what the tip was? Nothing. They didn't understand our wages were nothing, the tips were all we had. They just didn't understand."

Harry's wages, like those of millions of others during the depression, were irregular at best and not enough to make ends meet. Sometimes Mary held two jobs. It was during those years that Tom was born.

"I remember it well," she said. "I remember it very well. That was before they passed the NRA and then they had to pay you twelve dollars a week."

Mary had been well prepared by her parents to deal with adversity, economic and otherwise. They had prepared her as they themselves had been prepared.

Michael and Anna, her parents, had come separately from Galicia when they were both fifteen, shortly after the turn of the century, when it was still a crownland of Austria. There were many people like them in those days, coming to eastern Pennsylvania to farm its fertile land and to work in its mills. The homeland they gladly left behind was presided over by Franz Josef, their septuagenarian emperor who was trying to conserve the power of the Hapsburgs, even as the conglomerate dynasty he ruled slipped more and more into the disarray that preceded the Great War.

Michael and Anna did not know each other in Europe and did not even come from the same village. But they were both Ruthenian—Little Russians to the *hoch kultur* Austrians—and they both spoke Ukrainian. That gave them a special initial affinity when they met by chance at a wedding in Philadelphia. Anna, with her blue eyes and blond hair, was a striking woman. Michael saw her, pursued her, and during their courtship began to call her his *zlota* Anna, his Golden Anna. He would call her Golden Anna for the rest of his life, which would last until 1951.

Even though her parents shared a language and used it during their years together in Pennsylvania, Mary does not recall that they ever exchanged happy reminiscences of the old country or that they cherished Galician customs that they were anxious to pass on to their children. She does not deny her ethnicity but it has no real locus in Europe. Michael and Anna would understand.

In the years preceding their departure, Poles lived in western Galicia, the Ukrainians in the east, and those near the area where the two came together shared a purgatory of violence that the Austrian government was never able to control, not that it ever tried very hard. Franz Josef was far too civilized to attempt imposing order on a place that had resisted it for so many years. Ever since the twelfth century, Galicia, its winters fierce but its ground fertile, had been coveted by Hungary, Poland and Austria and it never did develop a national conscience that was accepted by all the minorities that bristled within its borders. Western Galicia remained predominantly Polish but eastern Galicia was filled with people who preferred to speak Ukrainian, although they understood Polish and Russian, too. Years later, when the family was more comfortably settled into the working class of Pennsylvania, Mary was told by Anna about the time soldiers came to their village, ordered that one of Anna's sisters dig a big hole, then shot her and her six children, using the hole as a common burial ground. Anna told Mary that the soldiers spoke Polish but there never was an explanation as to who might have sent them or why they should have massacred so many villagers that day. Anna and her sister Anastasia, who was called Nelly, thus found it not at all a difficult decision to leave Galicia for America.

As for Michael, his family had land in the old country and he helped farm it. But both of his parents were dead and he found that his older brother was stern, rigid, uncaring—a poor substitute father. It caused him to conclude, early on, that should he ever become a father, he would never make such mistakes. He would have liked to go to elementary school but was, instead, ordered to work in the fields, which he did. He did not even own a pair of shoes until shortly before his confirmation, when he was approaching the age of twelve. All he knew, really, was work. His labor was not even rewarded with a proper bath. Soap was a luxury almost unheard of. Years later, Michael would tell Mary that in the old country they used to wash their hair in sauerkraut juice. The poor Ruthenians and perhaps even the wealthy Austrians knew that the washing of hair in sauerkraut juice and certain other fermented liquids gave hair an uncommon sheen. But sauerkraut juice was never as fashionable as soap. Not then and not now.

Nor did they have a barn. The animals his family raised wandered in and out of their cottage whenever they needed shelter from rain or snow. Like so many others born into peasantry in Eastern and Southern Europe, Michael realized he had little to lose by venturing to America.

Golden Anna and Michael were married in Clifton Heights, quite close to Philadelphia, then moved soon after to Empire, Ohio, where he had succeeded in getting a job in a mill. It was only one of many mill jobs that he would hold. His wages were small but he wanted a family and Anna bore him six sons and two daughters. Of necessity, they moved back to Pennsylvania—a somewhat better job in a paper mill awaited him there—and they lived in a number of places, including Philadelphia, Kimberton and Phoenixville. Their circumstances were modest, but always much better than they had ever been in Galicia. If it was poverty, the family wore it well.

"When my father was living, our house was always a happy house," Mary said. "When we were little, he never sat down at the table to eat unless one of us was in his lap. He was a wonderful father, he loved us so. We always had company, we never knew who was going to come home to dinner with him, somebody was always bringing somebody home and it was good."

Michael had no alternative but to become part of a grinding, punishing, unforgiving work ethic that was, in reality, neither American nor European. Indeed, it was not an ethic at all— only an imperative to survive. It was an imperative that required extraordinary will and perhaps what is most noteworthy about it was not that Michael had such will but that so many others from Europe in those days had it as well. The work that Michael and his contemporaries did would become an important part of immigrant legend in America. It was a legend that was first the object of some indifference among those Americans who could take it for granted, and then, many years later, the reason for longing for the old days by a thickening America, whose political antiques took to asking whatever happened to all those quaint people who did so much work for so little money.

Michael walked four miles a day to and from his job in the paper mill so that he could save the twenty cents it would have cost to take the train round trip. He would walk there early in the morning on the narrow road that ran parallel to the railroad tracks, carrying his tin lunch pail. On a good day, if there were money, the lunch pail might contain french toast, cold, but filling and nourishing. If money were less abundant, as so often it was, Anna packed him sandwiches consisting of two thick pieces of bread pressed against some lard. Anna was proud of her cooking and of Michael and it saddened her to give such a man humble lard for his lunch pail. She would have preferred that he always have chicken and kielbasa and hot barley soup and thick sour cream and fresh hazelnuts and bread so rich and sweet that it made cake unnecessary. She knew what the Ruthenian diet could be. But it was not for Michael; he never had the money to buy such food. It could not be helped. And even in this, they both knew, it was better than Galicia.

Money or no money, Michael always loved the hilltop he had found for his family, not so far from the Schuylkill River where in those days, as now, there were stands of alder and ash and copper beech; where sweet buckeye, elm, cypress and catalpa competed handily with the stalwarts of the Northeast—hemlock, fir, holly, spruce, white pine and cedar. There were also oak, locust and maple, of course, and even a resourceful magnolia might survive in this part of Pennsylvania; the winters were not all that bad. In those days, Philadelphia and its big-city dirt and noise seemed almost as far away as Europe.

Their hilltop contained no subdivision. Nobody spoke of subdivisions. If you had asked them, they would not have known what a subdivision was. There were just a few houses, built by hand. With so many trees in an unspoiled setting, every home, however modest, was its own bosky garden. It was such a fine hill that even some rich people lived there, profiting both from the view, southeastward and northwestward, and the availability of so many men and women who were such fine resourceful workers. This is where Michael and Anna decided to raise their six sons and two daughters. Mary was the oldest girl and the second-oldest child, a situation that made it certain that if she had the ability to gain a sense of responsibility, she would gain it quickly. In this same neighborhood, Mary met Harry, who had been born in the same neighborhood of Irish-German stock. Here they established their own home, and here all of Mary's children were born.

Mary sits in her living room and thinks, sometimes, about the old days. Her thoughts are loving but always realistic. "We had a dirt road, no electricity, no water, and we walked down the hill to a creek to get water. It was good, pure water. There's a fence around it now, but when we were kids it was all open and we used to play in that creek.

"There was no well on the property, not at first, but my father got some barrels. We kept the barrels in the backyard to collect rainwater and that served for bathing and the laundry. I remember the rain barrels well, because each day it was my responsibility to use the water from them to wash the family's stockings. I did this after I returned home from school. My mother did the wash until she got to the stockings and those she would set aside and leave for me."

But for drinking and cooking, they relied on a spring that in those days carried good water to the Schuylkill, and perhaps still does, if somebody's chemicals haven't got to it.

It was down a long steep hill, a mile or so from their home. The children—Katherine, Mary, John, Peter, Joseph, Michael, George and Walter—had a little wagon, a child's wagon.

"It was made of wood. I don't think they had metal wagons in those days. It was a good wagon."

Several times a week, some of them, sometimes all of them, would place a large clean tub in it. Mary's parents were very demanding that the tub be as clean as the children could make it, since this carried the water for drinking and cooking. They would roll it down the hill and wait for their father to return home from the day's labor. Mary remembers him still as he walked up the road from the mill, about four o'clock every afternoon, a solidly built man, no more than five-feet-ten-inches tall, with dark hair and laughing hazel eyes, swinging his empty lunch pail, always delighted to see any of his children who were there to meet him, especially his two little girls. Mary thought she was his favorite. Given his way with children, it is entirely possible that each of them thought they were his favorites. He never talked to them about his work in the paper mill. Always,

49

he wanted to know what they were doing and how life was for them.

"We walked up that hill together so many times. Later on, he got the money so that we could have a well, right on our own property. Even then, though, even after we had the money to drill the well, I think that we ate soup every day of the week. I guess that I have never gotten over it. All my friends rave over good soup. But I have never been able to get excited about soup. Oh, once in a while, I like to have some soup, but it always reminds me that there was a time when that's all we had. We had chickens in the backyard, but we didn't eat them very often. Not like now. I don't remember that we ever roasted anything. I think I was a teenager before I tasted roasted meat. In fact, I think the first time I ever tasted roasted meat was when my sister got married. But we had lots of vegetables; Mom raised them in the backyard. She made her own bread, too. Well, sometimes she made it. Other times we'd get the dough already made and she'd make it from that. You have to remember she had eight kids and no washing machine. But mostly, I remember the soup. Seven days a week. Vegetable soup, bean soup, sauerkraut soup, pea soup, borscht."

The house that Mary lived in was warm and snug, more comfortable in most ways than anything that Michael and Anna had known in Europe. One reason is that a factory about a mile from the house would clean out its furnaces each morning and before they went to school, Mary and her brothers and sisters would go through the ashes, picking out coke for the furnace. They'd deposit their finds at home and then go to school. By the time they came home, Anna always had a good fire going in the kitchen stove.

"They spoke Ukrainian a lot of the time, and as you might expect, they could understand Polish and Russian, too. I used to say my prayers in Ukrainian, but I don't think I could do it now. If I go to the Ukrainian church, they say things that I can understand. But mostly, I've forgotten it all. You have to remember that in those days, if anybody spoke a foreign language they made fun of you, and so we didn't want to learn or use anything that would cause problems.

"I was very proud when Tommy took an interest in it. He used to hear my mother speak Ukrainian and when he enlisted in the Navy, the kid in the next bunk used to curse in Polish and Tommy listened for a while, then laughed at him and told him what he said, in English. The Polish kid was shocked and so pleased that Tommy could understand, since our name isn't Polish. I was pleased, too.

"We never did bother making Ukrainian Easter eggs. For us, they weren't fashionable. I shouldn't say 'fashionable.' They didn't paint eggs for Easter where my mother came from. A woman in our neighborhood painted them and they were beautiful but if we ever got our hands on them, we'd just break them open and eat them. We didn't know any better. We didn't know you weren't supposed to eat them, only look at them. We were so dumb to do that. The eggs were lovely.

"I don't want you to think it was all drudgery. You should have seen the house at Christmastime. People came all the way from Philadelphia to see us. We were never without company. And I remember that Dad built a cabinet in the cellar that he kept locked. That's where he put his whiskey for special occasions. My mother didn't like him to drink at all. Then my brothers got onto it and they used to snitch it on him and he never could figure out how they got in there, because he kept that cabinet locked. And he just laughed. My father was funny. He didn't know he was funny but he was. He had a very dry sense of humor.

"Sometimes, if he had an extra nickel, we would get an ice cream cone for Sundays. If he didn't have enough nickels for all of us, we'd wrestle, and the winner would get the prize. I used to get into those fights. I was a tomboy and I wanted that nickel. Mom would get angry—she didn't think girls ought to wrestle—but he'd laugh and smoke a Phillies cigar and watch us wrestle. Most of my brothers could always beat me, but sometimes I'd wrestle somebody who was smaller."

Michael poured everything he had into his family—his love and what he thought he might have got, had his own parents lived. He compensated to them for what the absence of parents had done to him. His affection for them was boundless, formidable. When his life was nearing an end, his courage to accept death was no less formidable. He faced his own mortality with the same grace and calm he had demonstrated when he faced the task of carrying buckets of water up a hill.

"Pop got cancer, he had it in his blood, and he didn't even know it until a friend of his came to him and said, 'Why are you getting those blood transfusions?' He said, 'They ain't going to do you any good, you got cancer.' And so Pop said if he had cancer and the transfusions weren't going to do him any good, he'd stop taking them. He stopped and he just died."

Mary still thinks about her father frequently. Her thoughts were very much with him during this final pregnancy, the pregnancy that she really didn't want, the one that gave her Lisa. Mary worked hard as she had always worked until about halfway through the sixth month. Michael would have approved of that. America might have grown lazy, but Mary had not forgotten how to work. That was logical. Had not the women of Galicia had their children in the fields? Surely, Mary could still work. But as it turned out, not past the middle of the sixth month.

"That's when it started. The pain. It was bad, bad pain. The worst I've ever known. I suppose it was mostly in my stomach, but it was so bad, it could have been all over. I went down there to the doctors and they said they didn't know what it was. They couldn't do anything for me. I walked around the house at night in pain. I was in pain when I walked and I was in pain when I sat down."

Arlene remembers it almost as well as Mary. "I have never seen a person breathing who looked so dead," she said. "She had no color. She had dark circles under her eyes. There were days when I didn't think she'd survive." The other children agreed with Arlene and there were times when even Mary, the indefatigable optimist, thought they might be right.

Her pain continued, fierce pain, as though someone had plunged a knife into her bones, and her doctor could not say why it continued as it did or what its cause might be. It was nothing that might be expected from a normal pregnancy, and the doctor had not seen anything quite like it before. Perhaps it would go away when the child was born, perhaps not. She could only wait.

Toward the end of her pregnancy, she began to feel the much more familiar and more modest pains of labor, caused by the contraction of the uterus. It was strange and disconcerting to be able to feel relatively mild pain under excruciating pain; she thought how lucky she had been in the other pregnancies, when ordinary labor pains were all she had to cope with.

And then, at about one o'clock on the morning of April 10, 1960, the water-filled membrane surrounding the fetus ruptured and Arlene drove her mother hurriedly to a suburban hospital near Philadelphia.

"The doctor stayed with me the whole time. He kept telling me to bear down and I did. But Lisa would not be born. She would not be born. And then suddenly she was born, and it was over. And the pain stopped. I suddenly had no pain and I looked at her and I said, 'Oh my God, there's something wrong with my baby's eyes.' The lids were red like fire. The doctors and nurses just looked at me. They said nothing and they just looked at me."

Chapter Five

The day after Lisa was born one of the hospital's pediatricians came to Mary's room. He was young, affable, sympathetic, and, it seemed, uncomfortable. At least, that is what Mary thought.

He was making small talk but Mary began to think that he was making too much small talk.

The pediatrician then came to his point. His voice was quiet, flat. "I have bad news for you. Your daughter was born with glaucoma."

Mary just stared at him. She did not understand what he had told her.

"I've never heard of glaucoma," she finally said. "I have had four other children and never had any problems and I've certainly never heard of glaucoma."

The pediatrician did not retreat. The diagnosis was quite correct, he said.

"It is a kind of pressure in the eyes," he told her. "What course of action do you think you'll want to take?"

"I don't know," Mary said. "How would I know what to do if I don't even know what glaucoma is?"

"It is a kind of pressure in the eyes," he said again.

In those first days of Lisa's life, there was a wonder about it. There is always a pleasant wonder about new life but the wonder about Lisa was tinged with fear. Mary looked at the little face and all she could see was the repose and innocence that only a newborn's face has.

"It was a beautiful face. She had lovely blue eyes. It was just that her eyes were swollen. But she was still a beautiful child. You could see that."

Maybe Mary could see it but some others could not. Diane, for one, noticed there seemed to be an unusual lack of interest in the baby on the part of the hospital staff. They were neither discourteous nor unprofessional, she thought. Only pointedly distant.

"When my sister was born, nobody would come into the room for my mother. The nurses wouldn't come in, you know, to take care of her. They treated my mother like she wasn't there because Lisa was different. Sometimes, they wouldn't even come in to check and see if she needed water. It was like she wasn't there. For a while, my mother thought Lisa was dead because nobody came in. Arlene and Jennifer and Jennifer's girlfriend and I went down to the nursery and said that my mother wanted to see her baby, that they should bring the baby out. Well, they did and as soon as they did we all started to cry."

And they said that Lisa had glaucoma. Mary was bewildered.

"I asked the doctor what he would do and he said, 'If I were you, I'd take her down to the University of Pennsylvania and let Dr. Scheie take a look at her.'"

Mary doesn't even remember the physician's name now but she does remember that he was troubled and there was a certain intensity about his referral; Mary knew she would not ignore it. Lisa was taken to the Hospital of the University of Pennsylvania in her third day of life.

The recommendation to Scheie was an appropriate one. It was an entrée to a formidable professional, an individualist's individual who was already something of a legend at the University of Pennsylvania, both feared and beloved by those around him.

Harold Glendon Scheie was an effective organizer and fund-raiser, a surgeon of note and a highly respected professor of ophthalmology at Penn's medical school. He had been born to modest circumstances in South Dakota, into the gray bleak penury with which Mary was all too familiar, then worked his way through the University of Minnesota, supporting his sister in nursing school in the bargain. In the early 1930s, while working nights in the busy loneliness of a parking garage in Minneapolis, he had met and quickly made friends with a young Hungarian who directed the Minneapolis Symphony Orchestra. The conductor's name was Eugene Ormandy.

In later years, after both Ormandy and Scheie became fixtures in Philadelphia, Scheie's colleagues would jest that it was not by chance that the young medical student would be attracted to an artist whose professional traditions, rooted in the nineteenth century, represented one of the last expressions of pure autocracy on earth. Such autocracy is a rare reality, a thing that symphony conductors share only with whatever extant divine-right potentates there might be and a few senior editors of very large metropolitan newspapers. A dozen years after his first operation on Lisa, Scheie would be a founding director of the eye institute that now bears his name. A commemorative book distributed on the occasion, written by his colleagues, would describe Scheie thus:

"He has a ceaseless industrious approach to life and is not concerned that this irritates many people. Dr. Scheie, at work, may appear to be a hard man, especially to his staff and residents; yet he thinks of these people as members of his family. He is generous to them with respect to finances but he dominates their lives. He works day and night himself and he expects them to do the same. Dr. Scheie does not permit his personal considerations to take precedence over his work; his staff is not expected to either. He is blunt and intolerant of mistakes. He is usually in a rush and those working under him sometimes feel he will not take time to listen to what they have to say."

But that was a side of him Lisa would never know. From

April 14, 1960, on, when she was four days old and Scheie was performing the first procedure on her, the basis for a new friendship was there. It was an important one to Scheie, rivaling, in its way, his friendship with Ormandy. For Scheie easily admired the power to endure adversity as much as he did the power of great conducting, and Lisa surely performed as well in her arena as Ormandy did in his.

Diane was there when Scheie first met Lisa and she saw that tears welled up in his eyes as he discovered what was happening to Lisa's face. It was a predicament he never really got used to. As the years passed, as Lisa's face became more and more lost under tumor, as he sensed what was being inflicted on Lisa in the street, Scheie fought back tears again and again. Scheie does not talk about Lisa tearfully, either to her family or to anyone else, but Diane was watching and she knows how he felt.

But if Lisa made him sad, she brought him a special kind of friendship, too. Within a few years, after Lisa began to talk and her visits to Scheie's office were depressingly frequent, they developed a little patter.

After the examination was over, Lisa always asked, "When do you want me to come back?" and Scheie always responded, "Tomorrow."

Then Scheie would give her a lollipop and ask, "When would you like to come back?" and Lisa would always answer, "Tomorrow." She quite captured his heart, as she would Whitaker's, later on.

In those years, Lisa was always an open, loving and trusting child, made so by her mother, her sisters, and her own natural ingenuousness.

Each year, in September or so, Mary would bring Scheie the last rose of summer from her garden. It wasn't really the last rose, of course, because roses have a stubbornness in their fragility and each year they refuse to be counted out. Mary had never read Horace but as an expert grower of roses she instinctively understood the wisdom of his advice: "Cease your efforts to find where the last rose lingers." Still, her rose to

Scheie was always a late rose, and sometimes it did not arrive until late October, although it might arrive just after Labor Day. It was the rose Mary chose to call her last one. She'd always wait until there appeared one special rose, one that promised to be more sumptuous than the others. The special people who possess the magic and the patience to understand flowers can tell when one will be a little more remarkable than the others. Mary could do this, and she could make a pretty good guess as to when it might be at its peak and that enabled her to make an appointment for Lisa a week or so in advance. She'd try to time it so that the rose would be on its way to peaking, slow bursting from the bud that had held it since winter, because she knew a budding rose was the most beautiful of all. Hard-as-nails Scheie looked forward to this ritual each year because he knew the rose would be selected so that he could enjoy its beauty for days after she and Lisa had gone. On the day that they'd drive into Philadelphia for Lisa's appointment, she'd cut the stem at an angle, wrap it in a very moist napkin, which in turn would be wrapped in whatever paper might be handy. Mary did all of this carefully, surrounding the special rose with greens and lesser roses, but always the best ones that she had.

Even at birth, Lisa quickly became the subject of medical notations that sounded alarms about her future, although the alarms did not always ring clearly.

Her first admission to the Hospital of the University of Pennsylvania is capsulized in records that simply reported that she was born at the suburban Philadelphia hospital and that "she had swollen eyelids at the time of delivery and subsequent examination revealed excessive tearing and bilateral corneal opacities. There was no family history of eye disease. Her mother was 44."

Neurofibromatosis strikes an estimated thirty to fifty Americans for every one hundred thousand born. And so it rivals multiple sclerosis and muscular dystrophy as a national health problem. But given the extraordinary variation with which the disorder might express itself, a range that might render it scarcely noticeable, individual physicians, even those in teaching hospitals, might go through a lifetime without identifying a single case. There was and is no neat and easy chemical test to determine who might have neurofibromatosis, which continues to defy those who would try to discover its genetic marker.

And so in their first meeting, Scheie did not know precisely what was wrong with Lisa. He knew only that she was born with glaucoma and this alone was more than enough to give him cause for concern. Glaucoma is the word doctors use to describe a buildup of excess pressure within that complex marvel we call the eye. Scheie knew that if he did not relieve the pressure in both her eyes, it would probably damage both retinas and both optic nerves. Glaucoma is probably responsible for half the cases of blindness among adults in the United States. What causes it is arguable, but it rarely occurs in children. Why, he wondered, was she born with it?

In healthy eyes, the fluid that lubricates them passes in front of the vitreous, which is the transparent substance that occupies a portion of the eyeball between the lens, the organ that refracts light, and the retina, the innermost part of the eyeball where the picture is recorded. The fluid then goes behind the iris, the colored portion of the eye, and eventually emerges from the pupil. In congenital glaucoma, the intricate system for removing fluid from the eye, called the trebecular meshwork, is faulty. The system, which is within the angle formed between the cornea and the iris, filters the eye's fluid and allows it to drain into a part of the eye called Schlemm's Canal.

Scheie's approach was to do a procedure he created—something called a goniopuncture, which essentially involves surgically opening the canal so that it does what all canals are supposed to do, permit flow and thus allow the pressure within the eye to be relieved. On April 16, two days after the operation, Scheie wrote to Dr. Frank Lutman, who had been the referring physician, and reported on the operation.

He said he was "amazed" to find that the escaping fluid was

yellow in color. "We are at a loss to explain this. The child apparently had no jaundice. Studies will be done to hope to find the precise cause. In addition, each iris showed a rather large number of abnormal vessels. Surgery was done uneventfully. Her anterior chambers appeared well formed yesterday. Many thanks for referring her." Lisa's records at the Hospital of the University of Pennsylvania also report, "The patient tolerated the procedure well and left the operating room in good condition."

In that single clinical report, he capsulized much of what marked her life: the ominous development of abnormal vessels, which would ultimately constitute a medical disaster, and her extraordinary ability to withstand the excruciating pain that would follow her many operations.

Lisa was discharged on April 18, with the recommendation that she be returned to the hospital in a month to make certain that the glaucoma was not reasserting itself. Mary did not need experts at the hospital to tell her that something continued to be wrong with her baby, who cried almost constantly and appeared to be in considerable discomfort. Mary was in considerable discomfort, too, and this normally vigorous woman was physically unable to tend to her child. Shortly after Lisa was born, Mary was admitted on an emergency basis to the hospital herself, suffering from acute appendicitis. Whether the appendix figured in the pain she had experienced before Lisa was born is a matter of some conjecture. Mary's sister, who lived nearby, took Lisa to the hospital for the scheduled checkup and, once again, Scheie found evidence of glaucoma. He had no choice but to repeat the same operation he had done on April 14. It was only the second of six such operations he would do.

A crying Lisa was awaiting Mary when she returned home from her appendectomy. Indeed, for the next two years of her life, Lisa would cry every day.

Neither Mary nor her daughters can remember a day when she did not cry; unrelenting tears that came from unrelenting pain and eye pressures that never seemed to stay down for very long, even after Scheie tried his best to find surgical solutions that would last. But they were not to last. The abnormal growth of tissue had begun and so no surgical solution could ever be a permanent one. It was temporary but it was all they had. Lisa had to endure the pain of surgery so that there would be less pain—at least for a while.

It was an ordeal that might have broken an ordinary family. Indeed, such things have caused enmity within other families. In this one, it seemed only to strengthen the bonds already present between Mary and her daughters.

Diane, who was only fifteen years old, immediately assumed the task of diapering Lisa. She was also principally responsible for teaching her sister how to walk and make the first sounds that might be described as talking. Mary had to resume waiting on tables as soon as she was able and she worked long hours. In a sense, those early days forged relationships that gave Lisa not three sisters, but four; not one mother, but two. In their closeness, Lisa and Mary became like sisters. But in Mary's absence, Diane became a surrogate mother. Diane and Mary hold their dual roles to this day, even though the original reasons for them no longer exist.

Years later, at a dress store in Norristown, where Mary, Diane and Lisa would sometimes shop, the saleslady always refused to believe that Lisa was Mary's daughter. Her suspicions were only heightened when she heard Lisa refer to Diane as "Mommyana" and she was further confused when Lisa called Mary "Mommy."

Diane was not only a surrogate mother but also Lisa's closest sister, not just in age, but in spirit and in personality.

"I am a very private person," Lisa told me. "There isn't any one person I tell everything to, but I tell Diane more than I tell anyone else."

That was reasonable for a kid sister who was so loved by Diane that after Lisa became three or so, Diane would take her on dates with her.

"When I went through that part of my life that kids go

through, the part that includes juke-boxes and pizza, Lisa was there."

By the time Diane was in her late thirties and Lisa was going through her most painful and radical surgeries, the bonding between them was deeper still and as Diane had become Lisa's confidante, Lisa became hers.

Diane was also a private person, she never confided easily in anyone, but she probably told Lisa even more than she did her husband, Mario. This was due, in part, at least, to his status as a workaholic.

He had been born in Pennsylvania and was thus a generation removed from the immigrant ordeal. But like so many Italians of the second generation, he was obsessed with work. If he had lost his parents' ability to speak Italian, he had lost none of their capacity for endless labor, much of it in construction and contracting. Mary's father never knew him but if he had, he probably would have smiled and questioned all this industry. Michael worked hard because he had to, just to get the essentials. Mario worked as hard or even harder because he wanted his family to have the "extras"—the material things that no immigrant family could ever have afforded in the old days. He would work to buy a powerful car, a huge television set, any toy his children fancied. Diane certainly was not averse to material possessions but Mario wasn't around nearly as much as she would have liked. So she told Lisa many of the things she would have told Mario.

But mostly, Diane felt she could confide in Lisa because in every sense of the word, Diane had truly shared the agony of those first years. And somehow it seemed to Diane that Lisa, who had survived so much, was, perhaps, the strongest support she'd ever have, maybe even stronger than Mary. As Lisa grew older, there were times when she felt that she could not deal with her own problems, even though she did. It was at its worst when abuse from outsiders came with so much intensity. All of her enemies were outside her family; all of her friends within it. There was never anything Lisa would not do, or try to do, for her family. And so, from Diane's point of view, Lisa had a depth of compassion that she did not expect to find anyplace else. And she was right.

In those first years, Lisa's crying during the day was tempered by minutes, sometimes even hours, of quiet. Nothing like that ever happened at night. There wasn't a night that Lisa did not cry, every hour from when she was put to bed until dawn.

On December 7, 1960, Scheie wrote again to Lutman: "Your patient . . . has just been in the Hospital of the University of Pennsylvania for another checkup. Her tension remained elevated in the left eye. I therefore did a peripheral iridectomy [excising a part of the iris] with scleral cautery. I will examine her again in about eight weeks."

At home, Lisa might stop crying, at least for a time, only if someone picked her up and walked her, rocking her gently. Diane did this as much as she could and when she needed sleep desperately, in order to keep up with her school work, Jennifer, who was a few years older and just out of high school, took her turns walking Lisa.

"There was a hallway light that I could have turned on in the middle of the night but I never did; I walked her in the dark. We assumed her crying was being caused by pain but we couldn't be sure of that. Or, if there was pain, exactly where it was. The only thing we knew was that she wasn't crying because anybody had spoiled her. She was too young to have been spoiled."

When Jennifer had a job interview or some sort of early morning appointment that required she get some sleep, she'd ask Diane to resume. Arlene, her husband away in the service and living in the little house in back with two children of her own, normally did not get involved in overnight duty, but did the cooking and was always there for emergencies.

When Lisa screamed in the middle of the night, the girls walked their baby sister around the small second floor hallway just outside their bedrooms.

Harry did not participate in this activity, feeling that it was better handled by his wife and his daughters. It was a feeling that would only grow within him over the years. It is not that he didn't care. It is just that he felt incapable of dealing in a sustained way with Lisa's problems.

"As she changed, I felt bad about it," Harry said, "but I also got used to it. She had a condition and it wasn't right but it seemed almost like a natural thing. It wasn't a natural thing, but whatever it was, I got used to it."

He also said he felt that if he became angry at her tormentors, or anguished about her condition, it might make him less effective as a supporter.

In this, there seems to be another similarity, of sorts, between the early childhood of Lisa H. and that of the Elephant Man. The available records suggest that Merrick's father abandoned his son after the death of his wife, who had loved and protected young Merrick. Lisa's father most certainly did not do anything like that. However, his role in her upbringing, especially when it concerned the reactions of outsiders to her, was subordinate to that of the women in the house. It was almost always the women who confronted the various manifestations of Lisa's adversity, not Harry. They were better at it.

When asked what he thought of the adversity Lisa faced while she was growing up, he replied, "I tried not to think about it."

And Lisa was asked how she recalled her father during the years of her childhood and through all those hospitalizations.

"When I was in Ward J he came to see me. I think that was the only time he came to see me."

"In fourteen operations he only came to see you once?"

"Yes. But he can't deal with that," she said. "He had a tie that I liked. I remember that when he came to the hospital to see me, he wore the tie. It had some sort of print on it. When he came to see me, he made sure he had on that tie."

Lisa tends to think kindly of her father and it would seem that his absence during her many hospital stays was not that important to her.

"I can understand why he wouldn't want to come," she said. "I hate going to see people in the hospital, too."

And so the womenfolk looked after her. Sometimes, during good days, warm summer days and brilliant autumn days, Mary and the girls would take her for a ride, frequently through Valley Forge Park, which was not so far away. During the week, it wasn't so crowded and they'd roll down the windows. The air was fragrant in the little roads that go by enormous oak and maple; past fresh-cut rolling fields and ridges where evergreens grew and where once, Washington's troops were in such winter misery that they talked openly of mass desertion. Twenty years later, Valley Forge would become one of Lisa's favorite places, especially during the middle of the week when tourists weren't in such abundance. Even now, there are times when Lisa will walk there with her sisters. In most cases, they don't show up all at once, as once they might have.

Usually, Lisa will arrive with just one of them to spend a few hours. But Mary never goes there without thinking about those early days when "she'd fall asleep, but as soon as the car stopped, she'd wake up and start crying again."

During these years, Mary was a waitress at a country club, not far from Philadelphia. Her wages were three dollars and fifty cents a day if she worked both lunch and dinner. There was a hidden fringe benefit in that the country club fed her, but it had no hospitalization plan to offer her. Her posted wages did not, of course, include tips.

"Sometimes," she said, "if we had parties, I'd make out pretty good and we'd come out of there with fifty dollars a week. But there were Monday nights we'd come out of there with a quarter tip. It all depended on how many people we had. It was better on the weekends and so that's when I tried to work, but I think the kids resented it. Everybody else was going on picnics on weekends, but not us, because I wasn't home and nobody else would take them. Sometimes they still talk to me about those days.

"But anyhow, after I started to work again, Arlene would still come up every day and make dinner. She was married, but Eddie was in the Air Force as an enlisted man, stationed at Plattsburgh, New York. There was no way she could be with him and so she stayed for a time in the little house, just in back of ours, with her two kids."

Scheie continued his efforts, never demanding nor accepting more from Mary than the minimum prescribed by her modest health insurance policy. He performed another surgery in February of 1961, essentially doing to the right eye what he had done to the left eye in December. Finally, in March of 1961, he was able to inform Lutman that her "ocular tension is now within the normal limits in each eye which is extremely gratifying. The peripheral iridectomies which were previously done seem to have been effective." Unfortunately, not for long.

Some doctors at the university, Scheie included, suspected early on that Lisa's problem might be neurofibromatosis, but the first reference to it does not appear in her records until fifteen months after her birth, on July 3, 1961, when Scheie informed Lutman: "We believe that we have finally arrived at a diagnosis as to the particular appearance of her lids. We should have followed this before, but it is probably neurofibromatosis."

The files are not totally grim, for they contain some copies of the correspondence between Lisa and Scheie, originals that Mary and Lisa have kept.

"Thank you so much for the thoughtful gift you left for me . . . Please know what a pleasure it is to care for you and see you when you come to this office," said one note from Scheie, written on June 18, 1966.

"Assuredly, the last roses of summer are not only the most beautiful but the most fragrant," he wrote on October 14, 1976. "I have them on my desk and they are very lovely. Thank you for remembering me in such a special way."

By 1979, Lisa and Mary, aware of Scheie's liking for fresh flowers, weren't waiting for the last rose and so they brought him a summer bouquet that July.

"Your bouquet looks very pretty on my desk. I will enjoy them very much, and even more so since I know you picked them especially for me," he wrote on July 20.

And on September 8, 1980, he wrote her: "Nothing could please me more than to receive a visit from my favorite young lady and, as well, some beautiful red roses (my favorite color). You are a very thoughtful person and I want you to know how grateful I am for your gift. I think of you each time I look at them, which is often, since they are sitting on my desk in my private office. . . . Best regards to you and to your mother."

Sometimes the bouquets were spiritual. Mary had masses said for Scheie every Christmas, compliments of Lisa, and he always acknowledged them. "You always have the sweetest thoughts and it is a great pleasure for me to see and care for you. . . . Your visits to my office are always the highlight of my day and I am eagerly looking forward to the next one. . . . I only wish I could do more for you."

Small things. Perhaps even minuscule. Scheie did more for Lisa than he thought. His little notes were much more than simply the innate politeness of a busy, sometimes brusque doctor whose compassion is surely the equal of his imperiousness. Actually, they represent several things. They were messages to a little girl who had scant communication with anyone outside her family. They were expressions of caring from someone who was not a relative. If a great doctor must be part actor, Scheie's timing could not have been better, for he sent his notes when almost everybody else had offered her little more than their indifference, their gaucherie and, all too frequently, their anger and hostility. Mary saved Scheie's notes because she knew he wasn't an actor at all and because they gave to Lisa the thing she would always want above all else: friendship with another human being.

Chapter Six

When Lisa was just a little girl in grade school, she rode each day in a yellow bus, as did the other pupils who attended her school, as did most of the boys and girls who went to school anywhere.

She was climbing down from this bus one autumn day and the driver slipped out of his bucket seat and followed her to the roadway. He had looked at her curiously for days.

He looked at her now and smiled and cupped both his hands around her face, tenderly, as though he were her own father.

Then he leaned over, put his face close to hers and said to her, softly: "My God, you are the ugliest thing I have ever seen in my life."

He quickly climbed back into his bus, fulfilled, it would seem, and quite ready to resume his role as the transporter of children, their paid protector in early morning and late afternoon.

She ran up to her room and cried. There was little else to do. She did not even know how to tell her family what had happened.

It was not a likely neighborhood for such a thing to happen to one little girl. No mean streets here, no ghetto, no barrio, no people with knives or drugs, no roaring traffic's boom, no big city problems.

It was just the hill where Michael and Golden Anna had settled, a haven, they had hoped, for their children and their children's children, and for spruce and maple and one huge oak, an oak that Lisa liked to climb with Nancy, a very nice little girl who lived next door.

In the days that followed, Lisa took the school bus again. At that point, there was no alternative. But she reached a point where she could not take the school bus any more and Jennifer watched it happen:

"My mother couldn't understand what was going on and finally one day, Lisa came home and she was bruised. Then we found out that some of the children were beating her up on the school bus. My mother didn't go to the principal; she went to the bus driver. She didn't know what he had done. She said to him, 'Why are you letting them beat her up?' and he said, 'She's ugly anyway, so what's the difference?'"

They ultimately made other travel arrangements.

Many years later, Jennifer's children saw "The Elephant Man" on television. At one point, where he was beaten, Jennifer said to them, "That's what they used to do to your aunt."

The children said, "No, no, Mommy, they'd never hit her like that," and Jennifer said, "Oh, yes, yes they did. That's just what they did."

Diane, who was first to know about the bus driver, remains very angry about what he did and feels that he "should have been shot."

Lisa does not remember it at all.

Diane and Jennifer have kept the incident within themselves because they do not know what else to do with it. But Lisa has driven it from her mind.

In the years to come, Lisa would seldom permit herself to react as she did that autumn day. There would be other tormentors, others who would attack and cut deeply. She learned not to run but to walk home resolutely.

If there was a need to cry, she would not cry.

If tears came anyhow, she would fight the tears.

If there was a need to speak about what had happened to her, she would not acknowledge that need.

It is not that her family did not care. They did care and sometimes they would wonder, talking softly among themselves, what had happened to her, for increasingly, as the years passed, she told them precious little about what had been done or said to her. Lisa was always a very stubborn little girl, just as she is now a very stubborn young woman.

Mary felt she could usually tell when something had gone wrong. But if she'd ask, Lisa would only continue upstairs to her room in silence, saying one word: "Turkeys."

It was only a comedian's word for a fool, a word she had probably first heard on television. To Mary and to Lisa's sisters, "turkeys" somehow seemed an inadequate way to describe somebody who was trying to destroy her spirit. But that was the only word she permitted herself to describe the people who shunned her, cursed her, sometimes even hit her. Lisa came home with some frequency and said "Turkeys," and when she did, Mary would always know that something had happened.

"I knew when they hurt her or when they said things to hurt her, I always knew. She had a lot of hurt. She never told, she would never open up to anybody about all the hurt she had."

And so, although Mary was certain she knew when things went wrong, she wasn't always sure precisely what had happened.

With all of this, neither Lisa nor members of her family think of those early years as years of unending emotional and physical pain. They think about her pain and her tears only if and when they are asked to think about it.

They do not feel sorry for themselves. It is true that the women of the family cry easily if they are asked about specific incidents in which they know that Lisa received abuse because of her face. It is also true that the men tend to become angry. But that is only if someone forces them to think about what some people have said and done to Lisa.

One day, for example, Harry took Lisa for a walk. She was then four or five years old.

"Lisa and I were walking down the street and a woman approached us with what looked like her grandson and as she got closer, and she saw Lisa, she took a newspaper from under her arm and she put it over her grandson's face. I thought, you bitch, I'd like to boot you right in the ass.

"But I didn't say anything, I kept on walking. I didn't say anything to Lisa and I don't know if she noticed or not. I suppose at that age, she didn't. I didn't do anything. It wouldn't have done any good to talk to that woman or try to correct her. It never does any good. People are ignorant and you have to forgive them."

Mentally and physically, the members of Lisa's family are surely within the parameters of what most Americans think of as good, hard-working neighbors. And so they tend not to dwell on the past. It is said to be quite natural and predictable to drive such things out of a healthy consciousness and so they have done the natural and predictable thing.

But there is another part to it. Lisa's immediate family know her, really know her, she is theirs, and for them, there never was deformity.

They all told Lisa, on occasion, that she was "no different from anybody else." They did not mean this the way it sounds. They knew that in her nonacceptance she was different. But they wanted the nonacceptance to stop. They wanted only for her to be treated as if she were not quite so different. That was never to be. Her differences were extreme ones and they are all on her face. The face of woman is not where her differences should be.

The standards that separated her from her peers are the same ones that separate whites from blacks from Asians; tall people from short people from fat people from thin people; the old from the young.

Members of racial, religious, ethnic and most physical groups could always turn to each other for support if they felt wronged in the schoolyard.

But Lisa and people like her have always been in groups so small that most of them face the schoolyard alone.

So Lisa was shunned by everybody and there were not enough neurofibromatosis victims for her to seek out as refuge. For her, the only sure refuge was always her family. It seemed she could not even count on that long-suffering pillar of patience, the school bus driver.

Nobody now recalls the name of the driver, if, indeed, anyone ever knew it. But it wasn't necessary to know him because he was like a lot of other people Lisa met in those days.

Accepting the way she looked became more than a habit with Lisa's family. It became their truth. Their feelings grew from and were expressed by their conduct; their honest conclusions as to what they should do so that Lisa could learn to live with ordinary people. They tried so hard to raise her as an ordinary person that it became difficult, if not impossible, for them to think of her in any other way.

"In a way, Lisa is at a disadvantage, being born in this family," Arlene said. "I think that sometimes we treated her too normally, too much as though nothing had ever happened."

As Lisa is no ordinary woman, she was also no ordinary child.

Mary recalls that when Lisa was a year or a year and a half old, she started to pick up words and seemed always open to strangers. Strangers almost never reciprocated. Mary wondered where it would all lead to and shuddered, for she knew exactly where it would lead.

Mary was shopping one day and Lisa was just a toddler. They were in that most perilous of places, a shopping center, the place where Americans convene to look at each other's jeans and cars and to buy more junk than they can use, abuse, discard, then return to do it again.

Two nuns approached her. They had seen Lisa, and they had a message for Mary.

"One of them said to me, 'Well, in a way, you have nothing to worry about because you know what's wrong with your child. But there are a lot of people walking around this store who are a lot worse than she is, but their problems are hidden. Nobody will ever know what their problems are.'"

The nuns could, by virtue of their experience, predict what might happen to the little girl with the warped face. But they could not have foreseen how Lisa's mind would grow. Proof of its growth is not simply within expressions of pride from Lisa's family. It has been expressed by much more objective observers. And those expressions started when Lisa was quite young.

In February of 1963, for example, Scheie received a letter from Dr. Frank W. Shaffer, medical director of the Developmental Center and School for Handicapped Children that then served the county where Lisa lived. Lisa was three years old, her visible problems were mounting, and Mary thought she had better begin exploring the suitability of whatever programs existed to help children with Lisa's problems. So, she had brought Lisa into Shaffer for an evaluation.

"I found [Lisa] to be a surprisingly well adjusted, very alert and inquisitive child who was at least developmentally at the three year age level," he wrote. That Lisa's good spirits and charm had surprised Shaffer did not surprise Scheie a bit, since he had always found her cheerful and well adjusted each time she visited his office with Mary, even though the reasons for their going were caused by problems that seemed to be getting worse, not better.

Nor was he surprised when he received another letter, three months later, from Dr. Herndon B. Lehr, a colleague with whom he had consulted about the possibility of improving Lisa's deteriorating face through plastic surgery.

"She is a very intelligent little girl and I wish there was something I could offer her mother for her," Lehr wrote. "Perhaps if her condition stabilizes, we can do something to improve her appearance by reducing the bulk of her lids and raising the bridge of her nose and reducing the bulk of her cheek somewhat. . . . I would be glad to give [Mary H.] any support that I can but it is a distressing situation at best."

It would be fully eighteen years before the stabilization that Lehr hoped for would occur. More bleak medical prognoses would follow. But in the clinical diagnostic reports, one finds that doctors were quite charmed by the way Lisa's mind worked, which was not bleak at all.

Shaffer took a second look at Lisa two years later, as she was approaching school age and Mary was trying to decide precisely where such a child would be best off.

Lisa "has a very pleasing, ingratiating personality and one rapidly loses sight of her physical appearance," Shaffer wrote, obviously aware that despite the growing disfigurement in her face, her mind continued to be very healthy.

"During my examination, she handled visual tasks quite well, including identifying of objects and pictures of a reasonably small size. On the other hand, her distant vision is grossly impaired and she seems totally unable to identify things on the Snellen Eye Chart.

"In general, I think it would be advantageous if [Lisa] could attend a regular kindergarten, but of course, this will be contingent upon her actual visual acuity and the ability to perform in a classroom, and secondly, upon the ability of her local district to assume this responsibility in education. As you are doubtless aware, there is a program for the visually handicapped. . . . I am not at all sure that it would assist [Lisa] to remain in a regular class."

Mary and her daughters were not at all sure that Lisa should remain in a regular class, either; they knew that ultimately, if the condition remained the same or grew worse, she'd have to accept the fact that she was visually impaired.

During this same period, Shaffer also notified Scheie that "at the time of this examination (2/22/65) there was a definite increase in the tumor masses involving both eyelids and also both right and left parietal [cranial] areas. Furthermore, [Lisa's] head size has enlarged appreciably, being now truly macrocephalic."

The tumors would continue to grow but in years to come, the size of her head would appear to be only slightly outsized. Scheie continued to consult with the best physicians he could find in order to help Lisa, and in the autumn of 1969 he turned to Dr. Thomas W. Langfitt, chairman of the Division of Neurosurgery at the Hospital of the University of Pennsylvania.

In a letter to Scheie dated October 23, Langfitt described Lisa as a "bright child" with a reported I.Q. of about 120. "She does well in school except for the social problems related to her disfiguration . . . the child is small for her age, and the head is slightly enlarged. . . . We will continue to follow her."

Lisa was asked to recall what she could about any or all of her intelligence tests and those who administered them.

"I think some of them [test givers] thought I was a moron," she said. "I can remember one occasion when the doctor tested me and made me put together a puzzle that was a square. Inside the square were nine other squares, three on three. Inside each square was a shape that popped out. For example, a red circle from a red square, a blue triangle in a blue square. The doctor dumped the puzzle, asked me to put it together and when I did it quickly, he was amazed. He even made me do it again. He said, 'I don't believe you did it that quickly,' and I thought, what do you think I am—a dummy?"

It seems reasonable to assume that the 120 I.Q. score, which is quite respectable and might see one safely through an Ivy League education, is a conservative number. It cannot adequately reflect Lisa's mental capacity. Standard intelligence tests measure mental capacity in a number of ways, most important the innate ability to reason and to solve problems. But reason itself is enhanced by wide exposure to life in its best sense, including its art, literature, poetry, mathematics and music. With her failing eyesight, culturally unpretentious background, and constant badgering because of her face, a standard intelligence test could no more take the measure of Lisa than it could a footloose child in Harlem.

As the experts tried to decide what would be best for Lisa,

Mary simply made the decisions she thought were best. One decision was that Lisa would attend not a school for the handicapped but a public school.

"She would have to function in a world where most people did not suffer from a handicap," Mary said, "and I decided I did not want her to feel 'different.' It seemed to me that it was better for her to go to school with ordinary children who had no special problems.

"I know she had problems at school, but I can't tell you what all of them were. Lisa would almost never come home and tell us anything. We heard stories that some children were treating her badly at school, but when we talked to her she'd say that it wasn't true, that she did have friends. She always said to me, 'You don't know what I'm going through,' and I said, 'Oh yes I do,' and she said, 'Oh no you don't, and you never will.'"

In the months and years that followed, as Lisa began to be hurt again and again, there would be times she would not even tell Diane.

But there were other days that were uneventful and when they occurred, she'd come home a very happy little girl. Indeed, many of her most glorious days occurred when she was in elementary school.

For example, when she was in the second grade and her class was preparing to take a trip all the way to the Philadelphia Zoo, the teacher asked the children to write papers in which they made believe that their partner was lost and they had to describe him or her to the police.

Lisa's partner, whose name has since been forgotten, described her as having brown hair and hazel eyes and he approximated how tall she was. He made no mention of the abnormalities that were beginning to appear on her face. The teacher told other teachers and the professionals in the school were elated. That was the side of human nature they wanted to bring out. They wondered if they could always do it for Lisa.

Lisa was smart, but her deteriorating eyesight plagued her all through school and she insisted that she wanted no special help.

She surely needed it, but consistent with her belief that she was no different and as good as anyone else in the room, she came to regard asking for special help as a "cop-out."

Arlene recalls that the family discussed placing her in a school for the handicapped. "For her to be able to cope with public school as she did—who would have thought she'd handle it as she did?"

No child in her class had a handicap as severe as hers. And so whoever worked with her might have to tell her if something important were written on the blackboard.

One day, Lisa didn't want to go to school because she had had some problems in a reading course. She had not seen the blackboard properly and she felt uncomfortable about taking on more blackboard work. She never wanted to ask either the teacher or the child sitting next to her what everybody else in the class could see. But Mary wouldn't permit her to stay away for too long—that wasn't healthy—and the next day made her go back. Soon after, Mary visited the teacher.

"The teacher told me that whenever she asked a question, Lisa's hand always went up and she always knew the answer. This one day that she stayed away, the teacher asked a question and nobody could answer it. There was a boy who was supposed to be very smart and the teacher told me he put his hand up and he said, 'You know what? I like it when Lisa talks because then we all learn something.'"

Arlene noticed several instances where, in elementary school, it was reinforced in Lisa that she was bright.

"The result," Arlene said, "is that Lisa never really accepted the fact that she is handicapped. In her mind, she isn't blind. She's the first to say that she's just as normal as the next guy and she doesn't want extra help, because if she admitted she needed it, she'd have to admit she has a problem. So, in a way, her feeling normal has helped her. In another way it's hurt her."

Lisa's independence may have worked for her. Her influence on other children with impaired vision may have left something to be desired, however, according to what Mary was able to learn about her one experience in a special summer camp, which she had when she was quite young.

"The Association for the Blind said they could send her to summer camp every year. She didn't want to go and I made her go. I thought, cripes, she'll get some friends, she'll have other people she can compare herself to.

"She went and she was ornery. They raised hell with her. They told her she wouldn't be permitted to come back because she led the other kids into things that maybe they shouldn't have been led into. The next year, they sent an invitation just the same and Lisa threw it away. I said to her, 'Why'd you go and do a thing like that?' And she said, 'I didn't like the way they ran the camp.'"

Lisa's Aunt Gert, who lived in Chicago but who used to visit Pennsylvania during the summer, said repeatedly to Mary, "Send her to a school for the blind, let her become a teacher of the blind." Gert thought that, among other things, Lisa might one day marry a blind person, "because he could only hear the sweet little voice she has and how she looked wouldn't matter to him."

But after Lisa's experience in the summer camp, Mary could never successfully induce Lisa to learn some of the skills that might be useful to one with impaired vision.

In the sixth grade, she had a young teacher named Robert Thompson. He was so good for her and to her that she still thinks and talks about him.

Mary doesn't really know what he did to make her feel as good about life as she did for that year. "He just . . . you know . . . he made her feel like a person."

Thompson, who has long since left the grade school, never forgot Lisa. He had dealt with other children who were ostracized for one reason or another, but he had never had a pupil with the potential for being shunned that Lisa had and he was determined that it would not happen in his class. The possibility was there because it was his habit to pair children off for a variety of projects and Thompson knew this could be the reason for yet more rejection.

"I recall sending her on a totally unnecessary errand to the library or someplace, just to get her out of the room, and I asked, as positively as I could, who wanted to work with whom. When I asked about Lisa, every hand went up. I didn't say anything. I looked at them. I can look at them and make them know that they made me very happy and that's what I did that day.

"These students had an understanding of people and they were intelligent. They weren't academicians, but even though they were only in the sixth grade, they understood a lot of things. In her attitude, Lisa brought a lot to school, though. I'd go into the faculty lunch room and I never heard any of her teachers say anything like, wow, yes, I teach Lisa and it is a tough job."

Thompson knew of many in the school who looked after her in their own way.

"There was the guidance lady. She said to Lisa, 'If you get upset, if anything happens, come and see me.' So Lisa had that. She had those things that she could do, those people that she could see, those places that were safe."

But teaching her still wasn't easy. Only rewarding. And sometimes, quite frustrating.

Lisa was already legally blind when Thompson taught her and he had a budget that would permit him to tape almost every book they were using.

"But she wouldn't have anything to do with it," he said. "And when Lisa said 'no' that was it. I thought it ought to be her choice. If there was a fire drill and she decided she didn't want to go out, I'd pick her up bodily and take her with me.

"Where I made my stands with her is if she came to me and said, 'These kids are picking on me' or 'This one's nasty,' then I'd say to her, 'What are you doing to try to make them not nasty toward you?' And then she'd have to say, well, 'I walk away from them' or 'I yell at them' and I'd say, 'Whoa, that's not the way to do this.'"

From what Mary and Thompson saw, it seems that Lisa, both as a child and as a young adult, never had as much trouble with small children as she had with adults.

It is true that at times there were awful scenes in the schoolyard. But within the closed society of the schoolyard, in which Lisa was required to be a regular attendant, there was acceptance, too. And many times the acceptance was immediate and genuine. Mary understood well that the small children tended not to care what Lisa looked like.

"All the kids always like Lisa. Kids will go to her right away because they know she likes them. She has no trouble with children, except for the ones that are taught to make fun of other people."

Sometimes, small children who had never seen Lisa before would stare at her, not in hostility but in wonderment, because they could not understand why she looked as she did. Lisa did not mind them so much; it was easy to understand the wonderment of such children, although Jennifer admits she occasionally got angry and told them to go away.

The scenes and the stares were worse in shopping centers, department stores, lunch counters, the forums for teenagers and adults.

Among the teens, sexual selection was beginning, a search for self. No room for Lisa there. And because she always seemed to know who she was, it bothered the teenagers even more.

Among adults, sexual selection had perhaps been made, and basic reproductive tests passed, but the search for identity might never end, especially among those adults who could not acknowledge that such a search was even occurring. The old adage, "Let them hate, provided that they fear," was operative. In the shopping centers they feared her and so they hated her. They feared and hated because they might be her and she might be them.

Thompson always knew she was bright and thought of her as

"gentle tough." And even though he saw her struggle to see the blackboard, forever having to ask the child next to her what he had written, he never thought that she ought to learn Braille. At least, not then.

"You do not teach someone Braille unless they are blind," he said, "because if you do and they can see, even a little, it shatters any hope they might have. You might just as well wait until someone is blind before you do that."

On one occasion, Mary went to a P.T.A. meeting and sought out Thompson. She was very curious about the teacher that Lisa liked so much.

"He told me that when he first saw Lisa, he thought he might have a lot of trouble," Mary said, "but then he said he found that everybody wanted to work with her, because she was so smart."

She knows that Thompson personally saw to it that Lisa got a guidance counselor who, he thought, would be more sympathetic to her needs. To Thompson, it was the minimal gesture of a professional, of a teacher who was always enormously proud of what he did for a living. To Mary, it was an unusual and unforgettable act of thoughtfulness, at a time when so much of the world seemed thoughtless.

"I can't tell you why Lisa remembers me the way she does," Thompson said, not very long ago.

"I guess all I'm trying to say is that school is a process that Lisa got through. She called me one day, years later, to say hello and I said, 'Thank you for sending your voice to me, dear.' I asked her to stop up and see me but knew from the hesitation in her voice that she would never come. And she didn't."

Chapter Seven

During the first eleven years of her life, from 1960 to 1971, Lisa underwent surgery eleven times. The operations, performed by Scheie as well as several others at the Hospital of the University of Pennsylvania, all involved her eyes, eyelids and face.

At their best, they were temporarily helpful. At their worst, they inflicted great pain upon her and the pain was all for naught, because the tumors continued to grow, slowly enveloping and destroying what would have been quite an attractive face, judging by how she looked newborn.

In an effort to save her eyesight, she had, among other things, three goniotomies with goniopunctures and she had two peripheral iridectomies with scleral cauteries. Her eyesight deteriorated anyhow.

She underwent repeated responsible but conservative plastic surgery to remove some tumors. The tumors stubbornly grew back.

She even had two exploratory operations within her skull because doctors thought they might find a tumor mass there that would somehow explain why both sides of her face were being attacked by neurofibromas. They found no tumor mass and no explanation.

Lisa's family knew many, many doctors. Some of them were brilliant, most of them were highly competent. Generally speaking, they also distinguished themselves by their compassion. It is noteworthy that after so much pain and disappointment, Mary, Harry and their daughters think badly of only one man. This particular physician, who had a rather unspectacular career in Philadelphia and whose name shall not appear in these pages, inadvertently did something that Lisa's family can never forgive him for.

After performing an exploratory brain operation and finding nothing abnormal, he informed his colleagues that Lisa would not live beyond the age of four. He did not know that Lisa's cousin, Emily, was a nursing student at the time and standing no more than five feet from him when he made his prediction. He said it with certitude. Emily told her father, who was one of Mary's brothers, with the result that he came to see Mary.

"I don't understand why you are spending all this money on Lisa if the doctors say she is not going to live past four," he said.

"He's only a doctor," Mary replied. "He's not God."

"Well, it's what he said," her brother continued. "He must know something. He operated on her, didn't he?"

"He doesn't know what's going to happen to her."

"It's what he said."

"I don't care what he said. Lisa's not going to die. She's going to live."

The brother died some years ago. He was a good brother and he meant well. But he thought Lisa was doomed; if she was going to die, she was going to die. He knew that Mary continued to hope that something would save Lisa. But Mary was only a waitress, not a physician. She had enough trouble pronouncing neurofibromatosis, let alone understanding it. He wanted her to accept the inevitable and prepare for Lisa's loss, not fight to perpetuate a life that was apparently not meant to be. Sometimes, Mary thinks about the surgeon who made the prediction. And sometimes, she and her girls talk bitterly about the doctor who thought he could predict Lisa's death. They never gloat. But their ordeal has taught them that a prognosis is

only that and that doctors do not always make the best for-
tunetellers.

As if the neurofibromatosis and the dire predictions were not
enough trauma, Lisa had her share of the bruises that might
accrue to any youngster. But for her, a childhood accident could
be quite serious.

For example, she was admitted to the Hospital of the University of Pennsylvania in April of 1963 after a kitten scratched one
of her eyes, causing it to bleed. She has always loved animals
and felt close to them. The kitten loved her back and was only
playing.

On another occasion, she was taken to the hospital, as ready
as she could make herself for yet another ordeal of surgery, only
to be sent home again—because she had a cold.

The files that thickened over the years in University Hospital
seemed to show nothing but her unrelenting decline.

In December of 1964, Scheie saw her and sadly made the
terse notation: "lids becoming more pronounced again, bumping
frequently into things." The files containing his descriptions of
her deterioration also hold the personal notes he continued to
send to Lisa, one of which said:

"I received your very lovely card telling me of the very special prayers being said for me during the Holy Season. You
always have the sweetest thoughts and it is a great pleasure for
me to see and care for you. I only wish I could do more for you.
My best wishes to you and your mother for a happy holiday
season."

In 1965, when doctors noted that her head was becoming
somewhat outsized, they recognized this as an indication that
the neurofibromatosis had invaded bone. Not long after that,
they also noted that "some proptosis" (bulging) had begun in her
left eye.

Lisa's family grappled with the reality of growing hostile public reaction to the way she looked. Scheie, who never made predictions about Lisa's future, continued his own futile struggle to
find solutions for a problem that had no solution. He was easily

as stubborn as Mary and he had no trouble at all pronouncing neurofibromatosis. With her encouragement, he looked for someone who might be willing and able to deal with the neurofibromas that were now visible on Lisa's face, especially around her eyes.

Early on, there was only a certain puffiness in the face, just a hint of the enormous tumors that would develop in the years to come. But her eyelids, which were not normal at birth, had worsened, and before she was even of school age, tumors were emerging in her upper lip. Doctors at Penn strongly suspected that the process of bone change would continue, although nobody could predict where it might end. Neurofibromatosis is as unpredictable as it is terrifying. The gene that causes it can create problems virtually unnoticeable. It can just as easily behave as it did with Lisa.

So, in 1965, Scheie sought the advice of Dr. Peter Randall, who was teaching plastic surgery at the University of Pennsylvania's Medical School and who was a skilled surgeon at the Hospital of the University of Pennsylvania. He had extensive experience and much success in correcting a variety of rare and serious craniofacial syndromes and abnormalities, as well as the common cleft palate and cleft lip, for which he had won international recognition. He had also proved himself repeatedly in rebuilding faces that had been grotesquely damaged by fires and in highway accidents.

At that point, Randall had absolutely no precedent for even considering the kind of radical surgery that Whitaker would plan seventeen years later. It simply hadn't been done, hadn't even been contemplated, as far as anyone could tell from the medical literature. Randall had seen neurofibromatosis many times before but even at this early stage in the progress of the disorder, he found Lisa's case unusual, as did his colleagues.

"It was unusual in two respects," he recently recalled. "One is that it involved just a face, not an arm or a leg or a back. I suppose that was not terribly unusual but it was quite rare to see involvement of both eyelids."

Randall's approach was properly conservative. The course that seemed to make any sense was to remove the tumor that was most advanced, then watch to see what happened. And so, in July of 1965, Randall removed neurofibromas from her right upper lid.

"As soon as we got through the skin, the material that we ran into looked like copious amounts of small intertwined worms," he said. "At that point, the skin was relatively free of this material though the neurofibroma was directly adjacent to it." It would not remain that way.

On July 20, 1965, he wrote to Scheie that Lisa had "pretty well settled down following the operation on her right upper lid. I think we have achieved a good result between lid and tarsal plate, but there is still redundant mucosa which is causing some eversion laterally." Basically, he tried to "debulk" her eyelids of neurofibromas and it seemed successful enough, although his own notes were ominous, indicating that her eyelids then were "grossly distorted . . . with tremendous redundancy of skin." Her lids were "everted"—essentially turned inside out because of the neurofibromas—so that Lisa had begun to tilt her head back in order to see.

Randall told Scheie that he thought the same procedure should be done on the left eyelid as well but that had to wait.

"Unfortunately, at the present time she has a rather nasty cough, and I'm afraid we're going to have to delay this until sometime in September. In any case, I shall try to keep you informed of any further developments."

Randall was hopeful; neurofibromatosis need not be virulent. Perhaps his surgery would prove of lasting value. But it was not to be.

"Everything that we removed seemed to grow back within six months," he recalled recently. "It was, to say the least, discouraging." Mary was discouraged, too, but she could not accept what her brother had wanted her to accept and she asked Randall to try again. He agreed to try and, in 1966, worked on the inside of the left eyelid, his approach as radical as accepted surgical procedure permitted in those days.

"Your old friend was back to see me," he told Scheie in 1967. "We've done pretty well on the right eye, but the left eye has shown very little improvement."

Randall informed Scheie in a letter of August 14, 1967 that Lisa "is not too anxious to go ahead with this, but her mother is, so I think they probably will have this scheduled before the end of the month."

Randall tried two more times in the next three years. On November 17, 1968, he wrote to Scheie after one surgery: "The progress on your patient . . . is certainly slow. I am not sure that we achieved very much from this last procedure."

The neurofibromatosis was indeed virulent in Lisa's case and on June 11, 1968, Randall wrote to Scheie again, his prognosis bleak: "I find it difficult to see much progress in your patient. . . . She has had considerable surgery and considerable tumor removed, and yet the overall appearance is still pretty bad. She is not at all anxious to have anything done this summer and under the circumstances, I rather share her feelings. Accordingly, I will plan to see her sometime next spring, and keep you informed of any further plans." But Randall never developed any further surgical plans; he felt they would be unavailing.

He knew Lisa's tumors were growing in size and number and that all she would have to show for the pain of surgery was a mysteriously pernicious process that would begin again. He continued to see her from time to time, but he could not, in good conscience, schedule more surgery. He believed that if there were ever to be a permanent solution for severe cases of neurofibromatosis, such as Lisa's, it would probably prove to be chemical, not surgical.

He told Mary that in one meeting, as he has informed the parents of other neurofibromatosis victims in other meetings. She heard him out but remained no less determined to find help.

"I think you've got to be honest," Randall told me. "There's nothing more difficult for me to handle than a person who expects you to do a miracle and then you go ahead with that expectation and they find out after the surgery that it hasn't achieved what they expected it to."

There was always a chance that one day the rapid growth of the disorder would slow or stop and that Lisa might try surgery again. Randall knew that each time anybody operated on a face, it jeopardized muscles, the functioning of the lids. Surgical scars might hide critical things from another surgeon who might try at a time when it made more sense. But that time would not come for nearly fifteen years.

As for his recollections of Mary's daughter: "She was a very amazingly cheerful, outgoing young lady." She would also become the most severe case of facial neurofibromatosis that the Hospital of the University of Pennsylvania had ever seen, or in fact, that most of the world's top plastic surgeons in the field had ever seen, as Whitaker would learn much later when he showed them the photographs he took of her.

In 1970, Lisa agreed to let doctors do a pneumoencephalogram, a fairly risky diagnostic procedure in which air was inserted into a tiny hole drilled into her skull, and then she was turned in different positions. The procedure, which has since largely been replaced by the computerized tomography (CT) scan,* gave her one of the worst headaches she has ever had. It was the normal wake of an pneumoencephalogram. But even worse was what it revealed: gliomas—small tumors with the consistency of soft jelly beans—on the optic nerves of both eyes, the nerves that lead directly to the brain. Such tumors have been known to follow the nerve into the brain itself. Attempting to remove them could impair her vision even more.

Worse was that an undetermined mass was pushing down on the ophthalmic arteries in both eyes. Another exploratory oper-

---

*Also known as a CAT scan.

ation was ordered and doctors found "dense neurofibromatosis tissue" in the orbit of the eye itself.

Surgeons gained a better grasp of what was happening but they did not know what to do about it. Scheie prescribed both pilocarpine and phospholine iodide to constrict the pupils and help in the absorption of excess eye fluid.

By 1970, he noted that she could see only hand motions from her left eye and that she could read only down to the second line of the eye chart with her right eye, giving her a vision of 20/200. Nobody could devise eyeglasses that would help. The bulk of the deformity now was such that glasses could not be properly fitted.

Scheie watched Lisa grow and become more and more aware that for reasons she could not understand, a lot of children and older people who did not know her did not like her.

"I suppose I was shaken up the most," Scheie said, "when she came to my office one day and told me that one of her class-mates had hit her in the face. I asked why in the world he would do that to anyone so nice and she said, 'He did it because I look so ugly.' That's quite a statement coming from a child."

Sooner than most children in a time when television had come to capture young minds and usurp their imaginations, Lisa began to turn to books. It is not that she did not watch television or like the cartoons and situation comedies that it of-fered. But her vision was deteriorating and there were visual images that she could not see as easily as did her contempo-raries.

So Lisa took to reading—by holding books right up to her nose. Her vision was failing, but a peculiarity of her impairment was that when she held books very close to her face, she could see words almost as well as someone with normal vision. Her right eye worked better than her left. It was a cumbersome, tiring business, but Lisa grew to love the printed word—novels, love stories, history, psychology, almost anything, including poetry. There are people—not as many now as before, it would seem—who simply read everything they can get their hands on.

Lisa was one of them. What books offered her was far more attractive than her reality, far more compelling than the shrill, scratchy, blurred images she might see, sitting twenty feet away from a television set. Ideas were valentines from writers she would never meet. She thus became an old-fashioned linear person in a new world where her contemporaries, and even some of her elders, had succumbed to pictures and slogans. As children normally did before the age of television, she could read and conjure up images in her mind that no television film can create for us. Neurofibromatosis robbed her of her face, but it never took her imagination.

Mary realized that her little girl was bright and this, she hoped, would help her deal with the years ahead. Teachers had told her there was hardly a time that Lisa could not answer their questions. Mary did not and could not share in Lisa's books very much. She was a waitress who worked long hours and she spent much time thinking not about poetry, but about how her daughter was being treated and how she would probably continue to be treated, if the process of facial deformity continued.

"We were shopping one day in King of Prussia—I think they had a Korvette's then—and Lisa was only a little girl and she went over to another little girl. She just wanted to talk to her. The other girl's mother pulled her away.

"She said to me, 'Mommy, why won't she let her talk to me?' What could I say? And the woman was pregnant herself. I never expected anything like that.

"I would tell Lisa that she just had sore eyes and that they would get better. Before the doctors explained to me what she really had, I thought that maybe she was allergic to something. She got worse and worse and we'd meet two kinds of people—those who would come up to her and say something nasty and those who would give her candy. I think people gave her candy because they didn't know what else to say or do. After a while, I told them to stop offering candy. It sounds silly now, but I didn't know but what the candy was changing Lisa's face. I didn't know and nobody else did, either."

Whenever and wherever Mary worked, and that seemed to be all the time and everyplace, she'd talk about her Lisa.

"I never knew but that one of them might know something, might have heard of something. I told them about my little girl and I'd ask them what they would do if they were me. They'd listen, my customers were always nice people, but nobody knew what to do."

Clearly medicine was not working. Mary turned to religion. She had never been a zealot about religion—she was far too robust and earthy a woman to appeciate the ascetics who had founded her Roman Catholic Church. And she had never really thought of her faith as something that might yield her a tangible benefit in this life. But she also knew that there was a body of literature that said that miracles had occurred through the church. A miracle was exactly what she needed. She acted with typical logic and vigor and she took Lisa to dozens of churches.

"We went to the Church of the Blessed Mother in Philadelphia, because I had heard that healing had taken place there. We just put Lisa there and the priest blessed her and we hoped all the time for a miracle. We hoped for something to happen so that the tumors wouldn't get worse." But the priests and their blessings had no more success than had Scheie and Randall and the others and the tumors grew larger.

One of her customers told her that she had a meditation group that met at her house.

"It wasn't a Catholic group. But we just met every week and we talked and we prayed. They prayed for Lisa. It calmed me down. My family doctor said she couldn't understand why I wasn't having ulcers or a nervous breakdown, but I explained to her that these meditations were helping. I always took Lisa and they helped her, too, I think. Not the tumors, but they helped *her*. I took Lisa everywhere. I never shielded her. Where I went, she went, and I was criticized for taking her with me.

"But I always told Lisa that she was as good as anyone else and that she had a right to go where she pleased. When they were mean, I explained to them that Lisa was my daughter, that she didn't ask to be brought here. Then they'd leave us alone until somebody else came."

No option went unexplored. Mary began to write to the evangelical Christian preachers she had seen on television. She wrote to Oral Roberts, who sent her a letter that started, "Dear Partner," and contained a small prayer cloth that Mary was to use as a "point of contact for the releasing of your faith." Dr. Roberts wrote, "I placed my hand upon your prayer cloth and prayed that God would use it." He suggested she write any request she might have on a prayer card he had also sent and that once he received it, he'd send it to "the prayer room where the Abundant Life Prayer Group is in prayer around the clock. They will lay their hands upon your card and pray, and I will pray that God will do all you hoped for . . . and more." Later on, he sent her a four-color picture of Jesus embracing a small boy. Lisa's deformity continued to worsen.

Mary wrote to Kathryn Kuhlman, who then had a widely syndicated television program.

Ms. Kuhlman wrote back, advising Mary: "Believe God's word and be assured of our prayers for the complete healing of that little girl's body; and with perfect confidence in His ability to answer. His power and in His mercy, we know that He will not turn a deafened ear to our cry or fail to answer prayer. Prayerfully, Kathryn Kuhlman."

Mary did believe in God's word but Lisa's face became worse.

She finally wrote to Jeane L. Dixon, a spiritualist, clairvoyant, syndicated horoscope columnist and real estate broker of Washington, D.C.

"I . . . wish I could be helpful," Mrs. Dixon wrote back. "How nice it would be if I had the time it takes to meditate on the hundreds who write . . . but regrettably I do not. The desire is there, but the quiet hours needed for meditation are not. Please understand.

"I appreciate the tremendous worries and tribulations which presently burden you. Seemingly, this is one of the hurdles that form life patterns for all of us, and one which God expects each of us to work out for ourselves—knowing that by so doing, we enrich our own lives and faith through personal triumph."

Although she could not meditate for Lisa, Mrs. Dixon did offer to pray for "continued Divine Guidance." She concluded her letter by thanking Mary for her prayers, "for I am always in need of spiritual support." She also enclosed a folder so that Mary, if she were able, could contribute to the creation of the Jeane Dixon Medical Center, which promised to "help children by endeavoring to cure many of the ills and diseases that afflict them, so their minds and bodies may grow strong and healthy."

Mary, hard-pressed for money, was not able to make a contribution. She was working hard as a waitress and just as hard at telling her customers about Lisa. At one point the members of the Plymouth Country Club contributed around nine hundred dollars to help defray the cost of one of Lisa's operations.

As Mary tried, as the doctors deliberated and the faith healers prayed, Lisa continued to go to public school, and for a time even continued taking the same yellow bus driven by the driver who had abused her. The driver now left her alone.

Lisa disarmed her schoolmates by herself.

At one point, they'd see her boarding the bus and they'd scream, "Here comes the monster, here comes the monster."

Lisa would get on the bus and respond, "Wooo, the monster's coming, the monster's coming, woooo."

"It was sad but, you see, she was playing a game," recalled Lisa's Aunt Gert. "They wanted monsters, so she gave them monsters." For a while, there was peace for Lisa on the yellow school bus. All she had to do was make believe she was a monster.

Chapter Eight

In the third grade or thereabouts, Lisa met Robert. He had lived just a few blocks away from her for several months, over a summertime, but she had not seen him before the September day they met at school. He was born in Norristown, but his family had moved only recently into the town next to Lisa's and when school redistricting went through, they found themselves in the same playground.

Actually it wasn't the playground. Lisa probably spent as much time on the steps of the school, at the rim of the playground, watching her classmates romp, as she did in their games. She suddenly became aware that a chunky, sandy haired boy began to quietly sit next to her, also as a spectator. It turned out to be Robert.

As her sixth-grade teacher, Robert Thompson, would observe three years later, when she came under his guidance and influence, Lisa had relatively good days and decidedly bad days. But there were almost no days when her face was not something she was asked about by somebody, somewhere. The children tended to appear cruel in the candidness of their questions about it. The questions were not always deliberately hostile, but that did not make them less hurtful. The adults, their ingenuousness past being even a dim memory, were simply hateful. When the children in her class learned to leave her alone (something the adults were never able to learn) they did it literally and Lisa was really alone—at least until Robert came along.

Lisa's face did not seem to bother Robert; they talked about lots of things that third graders like to talk about, but they never talked about her face. He never asked her what was wrong with it. He didn't stare at her. They talked of other things: loved and unloved teachers, the squeakiness of blackboards, the puffs of dust that came from chalk erasers that landed on one's nose, animals, vacation time, the depth of snow and its qualities for snowball-making, the heat, the cold, the wonder of seasons as they came and went—in short, the truly important things of life.

Lisa quickly noticed that Robert did not seem to have any more friends than she did and she couldn't understand this. There wasn't anything wrong with his face. Nobody ever called him ugly.

Yet the other children either avoided him or said things to him that obviously made him very sad. As Lisa's face seemed not to matter to Robert, whatever the other children found wrong with him remained a mystery to Lisa. She noticed that he seemed to cry more readily than other boys, seemed more gentle than most of them and more at ease with the girls than with the boys his age. But she found nothing wrong with any of this and so their friendship grew.

The children would dance around Robert sometimes, chanting, "Nyah, nyah, Robert-*a*, nyah, nyah, Robert-*a*." It was all quite incomprehensible to Lisa, then and even now; she could never understand what the other children meant when they called Robert "Roberta." All she knew, really, is that he was a gentle boy who quickly became her friend. There was another Robert in her class and they called him "Bobby," never "Roberta." But with her friend Robert, they always called him Roberta, never Bobby. So she called him Bobby. He seemed to like that.

Soon, Lisa found that when her classmates would taunt Robert, she would wade into the fray and take his part. Because so many adults and so many children had called her "ugly" and much, much worse, Lisa had developed some pat responses, among them, "Did you ever look in the mirror?" On a number of occasions, when Robert was being tormented, Lisa would confront her classmates, and demand: "Did you ever look in the mirror?" Then, they'd leave him alone, at least for a while. If they came back, Lisa would again intercede and order them to "Shut up and leave him alone." There were groups of children who, at other times, might taunt Lisa. But as she had already told them repeatedly on the bus, she was a monster, and a child tormentor thinks twice before he incurs the wrath of a girl who says that she is a monster.

Lisa and Robert were in school together for about five years, until the end of the eighth grade. They spent a great deal of time together in the school playground and another playground that lay between their two houses. They also took a few trips together on the yellow school bus.

"She stuck up for me many times," Robert recalled in a recent interview. "I don't know why they were so antagonistic. You know, kids like to tease other kids. Some of them become the bullies of the school and they think they know how to handle everybody. I always preferred to stay by myself and when you do that, people of all ages become suspicious of you."

Some of the boys in Robert's class felt they had good reason to remain distant from him. He disliked football. He thought it was too violent. He detested basketball. He thought it was boring; he found himself not caring whether a ball went through a hoop or not. Although he was big for his age, he never tried out for any of the sports that his peers took an interest in. He became interested in bowling when none of his friends shared his interest. That was something he could do by himself, a skill he could hone without being subjected to yelling or violence. He also enjoyed being a library aide—he liked stacking the very same books that Lisa liked to read—and he liked singing in the chorus. He also liked to sketch. He'd sketch almost anything he saw—trees, people, buildings, but he liked to do people most of all. It gave him much satisfaction but now, when he looks back on those years, he thinks his abilities as an artist were modest. Lisa remembers that they were quite good.

It might have surprised their classmates to know how much fun Lisa and Robert had when they were children. For example, there was a time that Lisa was a fan of a Scottish rock group called the Bay City Rollers. She talked about them incessantly. She even went to see them on one occasion, when they appeared at the Steel Pier at Atlantic City.

Robert took to teasing her about them each time he called her up.

"I don't want to disturb you if they're with you," he would say. "I suppose you have one of them under your bed and another one hidden in the closet."

"Just you never mind about them. They're beautiful. One of these days, I am going to Scotland and see the Bay City Rollers where they live."

"Scotland? You'll never do that."

"Oh, yes I will."

A few years later, Lisa did go to Scotland on a tour, accompanied by Mary. And although she never found the Bay City Rollers there (by that time, she wasn't so interested in them and so she didn't look very hard), she did find any number of castles that enchanted her. Most important, she sent a postcard to Robert, who by that time had moved to the Deep South with his family, far away from the hill where Lisa lived. Robert well remembers the card.

"Can you imagine? I collect postcards and there she was in Scotland. In *Scotland*, just like she said. Of course, I saved the card. She knew I'd save the card."

Robert cannot remember ever seeing Lisa cry or even becoming upset. Nor does he ever remember her complaining to him about the way others were treating her.

"I kept thinking, one of these days she's going to show them all." He also remembers that Lisa developed a very good imitation of Ed Sullivan, saying, "Tonight, folks, we've got a reee-ally good shoo."

Robert's family moved away, to Tallahassee, and from then on they saw each other infrequently. But they remain friends, even now. They call each other two or three times a year and there are letters in between. There is less to talk about now, less to share, because there are no more common experiences, only the past, and that is bound to diminish what two people have to say to each other. But they are friends and they know they always will be. Robert doesn't sketch much anymore but has become very serious about his bowling—he does it three times a week and carries a 170 average.

He'd still like to come back to Pennsylvania. "I miss home," he said. "I keep wishing we'd move back."

Robert wasn't her only friend in those early days. There was also a boy named Joseph, who wasn't quite as close to her as Robert but whom she always regarded as a friend.

Joseph loved to paint.

"He didn't do people," Lisa said, "but he could draw with pencils, he could draw with pens, he could paint, fingerpaint, model with clay. In the third grade, when the rest of us were trying to make ashtrays out of clay, Joseph made vases, vases that he baked and that were made so well that you could put flowers and water in them. I guess the others thought the three of us were oddballs.

"They were both sensitive to other people's feelings. They didn't go around hurting people. They weren't like the other boys, hung-up on being super tough. Most of the boys I went to school with were only slightly sub-human. These two were actually human beings."

And then there was Nancy, next door. They lived on a street filled with some rather large trees, the most formidable of which was an oak directly across the street from Lisa's house. It seemed to have been created for children who liked to climb. Its lowest limbs were accessible from the ground and its middle limbs, strong and healthy, were not so far away from the bottom ones. Nancy, who had no physical impairment of any kind, loved to climb the oak and Lisa learned to love it, too, even though by the standards of her school, her state and her doctors, she was legally blind. She reached for limbs that she could see; she clambered onto leaders that she had not seen until seconds before they came into focus. Neither she nor Nancy remember falling, at least not falling with any serious consequences.

"I was strong enough," Lisa recalled, "but Nancy could see and she could always climb higher. But not much higher. I could hold my own."

Mary was not totally aware of all of the activities that Lisa and Nancy were engaged in. One day, Mary said to Nancy, "I'd really appreciate it if you'd hold Lisa's hand when the two of you are crossing the street." Lisa heard this and gave Nancy a cold, knowing, dagger of a stare and Nancy never offered to hold her hand. True hell-raisers don't have to help each other crossing the street. That's what the stare told Nancy.

"Lisa regarded that sort of thing as a cop-out," Nancy said recently. "She is very stubborn and she never wanted any special help in any way, either in school or out of it. Her mother was worried that she wouldn't see cars, but I came to realize that Lisa has a sense of hearing that I could not even imagine having. You know, she'd say, somebody's at the door, and I'd say, nobody's at the door and twenty seconds later, somebody would knock on the door."

On warm and pleasant days and in early evening, before the sun set beyond the verdant gorge that soothed the weary Schuylkill, they'd ride their bicycles in the street, which was a cul-de-sac and carried no through traffic. And they'd wander over to a nearby park that is only a couple of hundred yards from Lisa's house and spend the day on the monkey bars or the Jack and Jill slide. Lisa never forgot that Mary told her she was as good as anyone and so that is how she behaved, although Mary would have aged much more than she has had she witnessed some of the acrobatics.

Nancy remembers that there always seemed something for a child to do in those days. By the time bushes and trees were greening, Lisa and Nancy could, if they wanted, wander into Lisa's own backyard to review the pieces of metal that would fit some model of something, as well as the things that Mary had put there—snapdragons, cucumbers, tomatoes—the stuff of life forever marching on pieces of aluminum and steel that Harry figured might one day come in handy in his work.

It was all a splendid stage for Nancy and Lisa. Nancy recalls that "most of the time that we were together, we were laughing."

Mary was always a firm believer in vitamins and since doctors could not tell her what to do, she gave Lisa a lot of vitamins.

"No kidding, if you keep taking those things, you're going to O.D. on them one of these days," Nancy once told her. Lisa just shrugged and they both laughed hysterically, the way children will do sometimes. If they had tried to tell their elders or anybody else why they were laughing so hard, it never would have seemed so funny in the telling. It is a problem that children have, sometimes, in communicating with adults.

Nancy and Lisa are still friends, but certainly not as close as they once were. Both Nancy and Lisa feel it. Part of it is that when they got into their teens, Nancy had boyfriends, boys who told her how pretty she looked, as indeed she did. Lisa had no boyfriend—at least, not that sort of boyfriend—and so they had less to talk about, less to share. But that was only part of it. It was inevitable that Lisa, who had once been so open, so loving, so trusting of people, would begin to change. Clearly, she had to change if she were to keep her sanity. It was an automatic thing. Her family and some people, a very few people, were gentle and kind to her. So many others were not. Lisa started to teach herself that not everyone was going to be like her mother or sisters or like Robert, Joseph and Nancy. And so a process started. But when it started, Nancy didn't see it for what it was. And it was as natural for her not to see it as it was for the protective forces within Lisa's mind to start it.

"I guess we began growing apart when we were twelve or thirteen," Nancy said. "I really didn't understand Lisa because I looked at her the way I looked at everybody else. We were so close, we had spent so much time together, that I didn't take into account her deformity. That's the way it is when you know her. She's so normal, so much fun to be with, that you just don't think about her face any more. To me she was just another person and my mom said to me all the time, 'Nancy, you're not being fair to her' and I used to say to her that, well, maybe I wasn't, but she wasn't being fair to me, either."

Nancy succumbed to the teenagery, Lisa to the reality that perhaps she was as good as anyone, but not the same as anyone, at least not anyone she knew. If one girl remembered that she had called last, she'd wait for the other to call. If there was no call, then there'd be no call. The pettiness of being a teenager was something Nancy would very quickly outgrow.

"After I grew up a little bit more, I realized that it was me who wasn't being fair to Lisa and that I shouldn't have expected so much from her and I should have understood what she was going through at the time. Instead of asking why is she treating me this way—I should tell you that we started to argue a lot—I felt like I was getting put down. Now I look back and I know I was a total fool.

"I learned a lot from her and she's still a good friend. Once, I hadn't spoken to her for two years and we were uncomfortable with each other for ten minutes or so, and then it was like we had been together for the whole time. I think I understand now what she's going through and what she's been through and I'll always feel a responsibility towards her, because to be a friend, you have to be responsible."

Nancy said that years after their school days together, she and Lisa got together at Nancy's apartment and had dinner, not long after one of Lisa's operations.

"I forgot she was still hurting and I bought corn on the cob and after I cooked it, it occurred to me that she couldn't eat it and she said it was all right, no harm done. If we were still as

101

close as we were in the old days, if she were still totally comfortable around me, like she was in the old days, she would have told me straight out 'I can't eat that.' Even so, I think we'll be friends for life."

Lisa still loves to think of the good days she spent with Nancy. And like Nancy, she knows they will always be friends. But she also knows that they will never again be able to capture the innocence of two children who regarded themselves as the same.

Early on, Diane began introducing Lisa to her friends. It was she who took Lisa to Disney World when doctors thought Lisa might have only a couple more years of any vision at all (they were wrong). She was the first to notice that Lisa was developing what was later diagnosed as "café-au-lait" spots on her body—an indicator of neurofibromatosis. She was even the first to notice, while playing with baby Lisa, that the strange disorder had spread from her eyes to her lip and that her face was changing.

"She was around two, I guess. I was playing with her in the living room and I turned her upside down and I noticed her top lip was growing. It was swollen, like someone had hit it with a board. The bumps were starting to grow."

As Lisa grew older and her face became more disfigured, she spent more and more time with Diane. They were constantly together; Diane even took her sister on dates. Lisa was frequently seen at a local bowling alley on Saturday nights watching Diane and her escort and joining them in the game. Lisa bowled around 120, which, she knew, "was not terribly good." Given her exceptional good looks, Diane did not have that many boyfriends. But those she did date all knew that Lisa might be along on a date with considerable frequency. Some of these people, most of them fifteen or more years older than Lisa, grew genuinely fond of her and remain in touch with her to this day. Those who were not genuinely fond of her were recycled very quickly by Diane.

Of all the women in Lisa's immediate family, Diane was

probably the most likely to lose her temper when children stared at her sister, as they inevitably did.

"There was a tiny girl, four years old, standing there, just staring at her and I growled at her, 'Where's your mother?'

"If I saw an incident about to happen, I'd talk louder or take Lisa in another direction. But sometimes you can't win. One friend of mine, a girl named Ruth, was so incredibly dense. Every time anybody stared at Lisa, or said something about her, she'd say to Lisa, 'Can you imagine such ignorant people? Do you hear what they are saying about you?' She was telling Lisa about things Lisa might not even have noticed. She—how should I put this?—handled things entirely differently from the way we did."

One of Diane's friends, Rita, still remembers their first meeting.

"I went over to Diane's house—this was before she got married—and Lisa was there and we took her shopping with us. We talked about stuffed animals and she said her favorite stuffed animal was a little dog that she had. At the time, my parents had a poodle named Sherry, which had just had a litter. We treated her royally—my stepfather used to chop up the white meat of chicken for her—but that didn't matter to Sherry. She'd begin growling, she'd have a fit if any of us even got near the litter. So we went over to my house. Lisa wanted to see the puppies—they were so young they didn't even have any fur on them—and before we had a chance to warn her, she went right over, petted the poodle, looked the puppies over, picked each puppy up and stroked it, and Sherry just let her. No growling, nothing. Can you imagine? The dog sensed something about her, I think, something that she did not sense in the rest of us, even though we always treated all our dogs well and we loved Sherry. But dogs are very sensitive and they have special feelings about certain people.

"After I got to know Lisa a little bit, it occurred to me one day that if she and I were sitting on a couple of park benches, facing in opposite directions, and just talking, I'd just think she was great, no different from anybody. But then I tell myself what has happened to her and I can't understand how she could be so unaffected by it, so good that she never complains about it. She just keeps on truckin'.

"I can remember sometimes I'd go over to their house and something had happened. Diane would get Lisa to sit on her lap and tell her about it. Diane would cry, she would cry constantly when she thought about what was happening to Lisa. But the family never wanted to fight. They aren't that way. They sort of felt, well, we'll go into this store and hope that nothing will happen, let's not have any incidents, but if they come, you just walk out.

"Lisa was a flower girl at my wedding, thirteen years ago. I found out that she always wished she could be a flower girl at a wedding, and when we decided to get married she was the first person we asked. She was terrific, adorable. We took movies of everybody, including her. She danced with some people and she had a good time. I had a couple of aunts who thought it was disgraceful that Lisa would be in our wedding, but what are you going to do with dumb people like that?

"When my daughter made her First Communion, we had a lot of people over and Lisa came, of course, but she admitted to me that the hardest thing was to come to a house where she didn't know everybody beforehand. Nothing happened, but there was this one little girl who didn't know what to make of Lisa, and before anything happened her mother went over to make sure that she didn't stare. It's not so hard to do that."

But it was hard for some people to deal with Lisa, even people who loved her. And sometimes, even for the people who were related to her through marriage. Jennifer's husband, Vic, was one of those people in the early days. Not too long ago, Vic and Jennifer sat in their living room and talked about those days.

"I didn't know how to cope with her when she came over here so I was rough with her all the time," he said. "I used to tease her. Not in a malicious way, not the way the others teased her. I teased her because I like kids and I tease them to get around them. I teased her a lot."

"And she was petrified of you," Jennifer said.

"Yes," Vic said, "she was always scared of me."

"She didn't like you at all," Jennifer said.

"Well, she did in a way. . . ."

"You were always hollering when you were kidding. . . ."

"I could not handle it. Just like when I was down at the hospital after an operation, I could not handle it. The others were there, but I was in and out of that hospital room four or five times. I couldn't look her straight in the face. When she was real little, when she had that first brain operation, I used to be down at the hospital all the time. I'd wheel her up and down the halls and I had a ball with her."

"Yes, when she was real little, you used to make her laugh."

"I guess it was my way. I guess, I don't know. But I can't forget what happened later, when she was so scared of me. She's not as much around us now, but I am sorry that I did this to her." Vic was uncomfortable with Lisa's occasional candor about how life was going for her.

Once, she was at his house and he noticed there were bruises on her arm.

"Where did you get those?" he asked her.

"My playmates beat me up."

"My God, why would anybody do that?"

"Because I'm ugly."

Vic feels that he gets along with Lisa "all right" now, but he still has problems.

"We went to that party," he said, referring to a recent family event, "and I can't look her straight in the face. I don't know what to say when I look at her. I always say something like, 'How are you feeling?,' that's all. When she was in the hospital, I'd walk over to her bed but I couldn't look at her face, I guess because I was scared that I was going to break down. I thought, I'm a man, I'm not supposed to break down, right? You don't do that in this country. My grandparents, they were Sicilian, and they used to cry and there was nothing to it, they felt good. But with me, it's different."

Vic was never afraid that he would "catch" whatever Lisa has or that she would somehow infect his children with it. He knows that Lisa is very bright and he even knows that she understands what is going on in his head. But he could never be just her friend or her confidant, as his wife could be. Lisa brought out something else in him, as it seems to in almost all men.

"If we went shopping anywhere, I was always ready to fight with somebody. I'd look at 'em, and I knew they were looking at her and thinking you rotten pig, or something like that, and I was ready to start fighting. It wasn't even my kid, but I still felt, hey, this kid's with me, it's my sister-in-law. And they were looking at her like she's nothing. You know, she's only a kid. I was always afraid somebody would say something to hurt her."

"Most men can't stand that sort of rejection, they just can't stand it," Jennifer said.

Jennifer thought about her sister during the first years.

"She was just unbelievable, she gave everybody the benefit of the doubt, she would never complain about being hurt and I suppose she hollered at us more than she did other people.

"Remember, Vic? Remember when we went to the fair in Norristown? We lived in our apartment then and we took her to this fair and we put her on a hobby horse or some such thing. There were two older ladies, they were so ignorant, so disgusting, they just kept staring. Didn't they talk to us, Vic?"

"Yeah, I remember. They were trying to talk to us."

"It wasn't just 'What's wrong with her?' because you don't mind people saying that kind of stuff. It's when they question why you even have her with you. I don't even remember exactly what they said but I know I was really mad, I was crying and we had to leave 'cause I couldn't take any more. I wanted to smack them. If they only stared it was one thing, but sometimes a crowd would follow us and the kids would laugh and point and stuff like that. I didn't mind the kids as much as the adults."

"I feel that way, too," Vic said. "You'd think the adults would know better."

"It used to aggravate me," Jennifer added. "I used to cry. I'm used to it now. Over the years, I got to the point where I said to myself, 'Hey, you're the one with the problem, not her.' But my daughter, little Jennifer, she's not used to it and she couldn't understand why kids would come and stare at her aunt. We were in the Plymouth Meeting Mall and Lisa was on the outside and I was holding her arm because there are so many people and I didn't want her to walk into anybody, they move so fast in those malls. Anyway, this workman came up and he said, 'There ain't no Halloween now, is there?' I wanted to smack him but we just kept walking.

"There are a lot of schools around here for the handicapped and my mother took her to some of them, thinking that she might get special attention, so that the abuse that was in the public schools might stop. But after a psychiatrist talked to the two of them, he said they didn't need a special school because Lisa was mentally balanced. She had no problems, because of the way my mother raised her. Lisa will never admit that," she added, laughing.

"I remember when we were little, long before Lisa was ever born, we'd go to church, or we'd be in the car and we'd see retarded people or strange-looking people and we'd say, 'Mommy, look at that man,' and she'd say, 'Don't you ever make fun of somebody like that because you never know what's going to happen to you.' My mother was always the one with compassion. She never made fun of anybody and she would put herself out for everybody. Her friends would say to her, 'Mary, you're too nice, people are taking advantage of you,' and she'd always say, 'That's the way I am, what am I going to do?'

"Once, before Vic and I got married, we came home one night and she was up, waiting for us. She always waited up for us. I was drunk. It was the first time in my life that I was drunk. I figured, 'This is the day you're going to get killed,' and she said, 'I don't have to holler at you. You're suffering enough, just the way you are.' She just laughed and thought it was funny."

Jennifer recalls that as Lisa was growing up and she and Vic would visit Mary at home from time to time, they'd notice that the tumors were growing on Lisa's face, and on the way home they'd talk about it, talk about the way Mary and Diane were coping with it. Friends noticed it, too.

"After her second brain operation," Rita said, "and they shaved all of Lisa's hair off to do it, Diane went out and had her head shaved, too. I don't think she had more than an inch of hair where it was at its longest. And then when Lisa came home from the hospital, Diane showed her her own head and said they should have a race, to see who could grow hair back the fastest. I thought that was kind of nice."

Chapter Nine

Philadelphia's finest surgeons, among the best in the country, had practiced their art but neurofibromatosis had no respect for it; the tumors on Lisa's face continued to grow. Catholics, once they learned from Mary and her daughters about the plight of the little girl who had suffered so much, prayed constantly, hoping for divine intercession. The tumors grew larger. Ordinary Protestants prayed with ordinary Catholics and with famous evangelical Protestants, some of them internationally known television personalities, men and women who drew huge throngs of the faithful wherever they went. These famous Christians sent letters of comfort, promising their prayers, too. The tumors grew larger still.

Lisa's family was frustrated, paralyzed. It did not repel them that Lisa's face was not "normal." But they knew that it did not really matter what their value system was. More important, by far, were the values of strangers, of people they had never met and might not want to meet, even if they could. Mary had always taught her children that strangers were only friends, once removed. Now it was clear to them that Lisa would have much trouble in the future with men, women and children who did not know her—could not know her—as they did. That meant that Lisa faced an existence of harrowing loneliness, a sterile world where her very womanhood might not be permitted to dawn, where strangers would forever remain strangers.

And so from Mary's point of view, it was the logical order of things to look for new solutions, solutions that lie outside of conventional and unconventional medicine, outside of traditional and evangelical religion, beyond whatever power there was in the compassion and decency that a few strangers showed to Lisa on rare occasions.

One day, after work, Mary went to a faith healer she had heard about from one of her customers. It had been nearly fourteen years since her youngest daughter had been born. Surely, under the circumstances, no one could fault Mary for consulting a faith healer about Lisa. The healer agreed to pray for Lisa. But he thought there might be another good approach, as well.

"Have you tried working on her feet?" the healer asked Mary.

"I don't know what you mean. How should I work on her feet?"

"There is a way," the healer replied. "Not my way. A kind of massage. It may work."

The faith healer told her the method was called reflexology, an ancient approach to healing developed by the Chinese but far less known than its more dramatic cousin, acupuncture. Mary had never heard of it. But her younger brother, Walter, said he thought he had heard of it. He was a steelworker up country and a man he worked with had a wife who had gone to a reflexologist.

The reflexologist was a woman named Doris, who told Mary that she had learned her approach from her uncle. She explained that it involved "compression massages" to the feet that might cure or prevent various diseases by restoring the body to its natural harmony.

Reflexology, Mary soon learned, was a discipline of maps as well as massage. And most all of the maps were of the feet. It seemed to her that reflexology was by any reasonable measure a mating of Chinese wisdom with the message in the old black spiritual, which advised us that the "knee bone's connected to the thigh bone," except that the linkages were measured from and within the feet. Reflexology promised that pressure applied to the underside of the left big toe would clear the sinuses; the base of the second toe held the key to better eyesight. Sore thighs, sore knees and sore hips could be relieved by massaging the underside of the left foot just north of the heel; and stomach aches could be banished by intense pressure applied to the ball of the left foot.

The right foot offered its own linkages to the ears, lungs, neck, throat, tonsils, bladder, colon and other parts of the body.

The promises made over the millennia by Chinese healers have never been taught at the Medical School of the University of Pennsylvania nor in most of the major medical schools in this country. Many American doctors have never even heard of it. But it is not totally alien to American academia. At least one branch of the State University of New York—the College at New Paltz—recently offered an eight-session course in reflexology for forty dollars. The students who took it, none of them doctors, were taught compression massage and how to create a "map" of a classmate's foot.

Mary and Lisa visited Doris and Doris worked on both of them. She started with Mary, who wanted to be sure that the approach was safe before allowing Lisa to try it. Mary soon learned that this was not a gentle part of the art of healing, this reflexology. The compression massages were aptly named. The hands of the reflexologist had to be powerful and much power was exerted; muscle and tissue were kneaded, squeezed, pressed and compacted. The pain resulting from the massage was intense but for Mary, at that place and time in her life, it seemed to work.

"I was working so hard at that time that I felt my whole body was breaking down," Mary said. "But she started working on me and, for me, it worked. After she got me straightened out, I could walk anywhere and my aches and pains were gone."

Then it was Lisa's turn. Her tolerance of the treatment was nowhere as great as Mary's and she winced as Doris's hands applied pressure to various parts of her feet in an effort to find the linkage that would banish the tumors. The treatment did not begin auspiciously; Lisa still recalls that she became ill and spent most of the next two weeks in bed. She remembers hurting and having a runny nose. Doris was not immediately successful, but that was no reason to assume the linkage was not there or that it could not be found if a care giver were patient enough, adept enough. But it might take a lot of time. Doris sincerely believed in what she was doing and she encouraged Mary to return with Lisa. Mary agreed and for the next year and a half, Doris worked on Lisa's feet every week. She charged only five dollars a visit—the same rate that Harold Scheie always charged Lisa when he saw her in his clinic.

As the months went on, Doris thought she saw in Mary another healer, another who might continue the reflexologist's tradition. She taught reflexology to Mary, and Mary thus became able to try it at home on Lisa, although she was well aware by this time that it had had no beneficial effect on diminishing the neurofibromatosis. But that does not mean it had no worth at all.

Lisa recalls that the massages hurt her but that somehow, she thought she felt better afterward. Hour after hour after hour, Mary rubbed and kneaded Lisa's feet. For years she did this. After each treatment, she would look at her daughter's face anxiously, hoping that somehow, something within Lisa would be triggered that would reverse the process. But for Mary, like Doris, there was no linkage, it seemed; the irreversible would not be reversed. The ancient Chinese could be forgiven; they invented their art three thousand years before the science of genetics was established. But ancient Chinese reflexology had its place in twentieth-century Pennsylvania. The treatments were another way for a loving mother to touch her daughter and reassure her, as only touching will do, that there was hope, that something was being done.

"I suppose that I was an idiot to let her do the massages," Lisa said, years later. "The massages hurt. But as I look back on them, I have to say that they also helped. I can't tell you precisely how—they certainly didn't do anything for my neurofibromatosis. We knew we didn't have a 'cure' for that. But I remember that I once got a foot massage for a sore neck and it worked."

Every once in a while, even after a new generation of surgeons entered Lisa's life, Mary would still give Lisa an occasional reflexology treatment. And she also gave them to her other three daughters. They all seem to be in agreement that for a lot of little aches and pains, and even for some big ones, the massages given them by their mother were quite effective.

During the period that Mary was learning reflexology and noting its lack of effect on the neurofibromatosis, she never stopped looking for other approaches. At one point, she thought that perhaps a more expert massage might help and so she took Lisa to several chiropractors, who were recommended to her by her customers in the restaurant.

One of them who was supposed to be especially good was a long way up country.

"He put her legs together and looked at her feet to see if her body was out of line," Mary recalled. "He looked at Lisa and he looked at me and he said, 'Her body isn't out of line and she doesn't need an adjustment.' He asked for payment of five dollars and Lisa said to him, 'Doc, do you mean to tell me that you are going to charge my mommy for something that you didn't do?' He said, 'Yes, you took my time, didn't you?' Lisa said, 'Well, I only lay down. That didn't take much time.' He was shocked and she didn't like him so we never went back."

Mary also took Lisa to quite a number of other doctors recommended by her customers, who prescribed garlic pills and an interminable assortment of vitamins and herbs.

But tumor always resisted the reflexologist's ancient cure, as well as the cures offered by chiropractors and vitamin specialists and natural food experts—just as it had the efforts of surgeons, the prayers of ordinary Protestants and Catholics, the prayers of extraordinary evangelists and faith healers.

With all of this, everyday life went on.

Scholastically, Lisa was giving a good account of herself in the upper grades of the public schools she attended, considering her slowly deteriorating eyesight, which made it always difficult and sometimes impossible for her to see what was written on blackboards. Mary saved her report cards, proud of what they represented. In the ninth grade, she received an A in American culture, B's in science, physical education and in elementary guitar lessons, and C's in English and elementary algebra. By the next year, she had boosted English to an A for all four marking periods, but fell to C work in both American culture and physical education and managed only a D in Spanish. Her school records for that year say that she was never late, but was absent for medical reasons for seventeen days. By the time she was a senior, she had increased her final average to three A's, four B's and only one C for the year. Her best courses were in motion pictures, contemporary living and music appreciation; her worst, in which she got her C, was accounting. She wasn't afraid of it, only bored by it. She loved to use numbers in other, less abstract ways. She got an A-minus in a term paper entitled "An Interesting Comparison of Supermarket Prices on a Variety of Products," in which she went to five markets and compared the prices on fifteen items, concluding that "no store is consistently cheaper than another."

In her senior year, she was absent nineteen times and was tardy just once, in the final marking period before graduation.

The music appreciation course was especially important to Lisa. She had always liked popular music—the records of Crosby, Stills and Nash; Johnny Mathis; Nat King Cole and, of course, the Bay City Rollers. Then came the music course and discovery of Johann Sebastian Bach. Her teacher provided her with a summary explanation of contrapuntal music. But she would have liked Bach without explanation because more than anything else she had ever heard, it soothed her. In a disordered world that had long ago gone mad and grown hateful and irrational toward her, Bach expressed the best of humankind, its sanity, its rival ability to be orderly, logical. There was precious little money for buying albums, but one day in a supermarket with Mary, Lisa found a classical album she could afford: Bach's Brandenburg Concertos no. 2 and no. 6 and the Clavier Concerto in D-minor. The label advised that the record was part of Funk & Wagnalls' "Family Library of Great Music," and was on special sale for 99 cents, midway between produce and poultry. It was, in fact, the only Bach in the whole grocery store and Lisa did not hesitate. From that day on, it became normative for her to end an interlude with the Bay City Rollers with a Bach concerto.

As her peers became addicted to "I Love Lucy" reruns, Lisa developed in another direction. There was much about television that did not suit her. If the situation comedies and the mawkish melodramas of television were designed to render visually and orally the world that most Americans wanted to see and hear, a gossamer stage where they could view (with a little imagination) themselves or people very much like themselves, Lisa found little in them that helped her own dreams along. There was no room in situation comedies for her. Television's unrelenting emphasis on the very standards embraced by most of the adolescents who had rejected her, represented something from which she needed frequent respite.

She never totally abandoned television, but she also became a reader.

If there was a developing cloudy veil of tumor and scar tissue and neurofibroma compromising her view of the commonplace world that lay so totally outside of her, she learned to use it to advantage. There was a jail in Norristown, a big building with two towers in front. To her, it represented what a British castle ought to look like and when she could, she'd go and look at it.

She also developed an interest in the Philadelphia Flyers ("I don't understand why. Hockey is a violent game, I don't like violence but I do like the Flyers"); the human voice and speech pathology ("Did you know that Tom Brokaw speaks with a dark '1'?); candy (especially a calorific thing called "Peanut Chews");

zeps (a kind of Pennsylvania Italian sandwich and quite formidable); hoagies (another sandwich, rivaling zeps); shopping for bargains with her sisters and her mother; ballet; small animals, especially kittens and puppies; and above all, her privacy.

Even in her privacy, Lisa remained surprisingly open. It is a trait she shares with her sisters, one they inherited from Mary. Lisa's openness toward others continued throughout her school years, although she constantly had to tailor it. To be open all the time to everyone was to be vulnerable to rejection and there had already been too much of that. In grade school, Valentine's Day, for example, had become a source of anxiety for the family in a year that might well have many anxious days. If there were thirty children in the class, most of them would receive a valentine from everybody else in the class. But Lisa received seven valentines one year, only one another time, and there was one year when she received no valentines at all. She counted the valentines she received, treasured them, saved them for years. But her heart wept for the valentines that never arrived. Lisa's family was mindful that Lisa could very easily become embittered about what life had not given her and there were specific occasions when they encouraged her to try to do more of the things that other young people were doing. One such occasion came in 1978 with the junior prom.

Lisa had not thought very much about the junior prom. She well understood that she could not afford to indulge in the daydreams of ordinary teenagers. She had not been asked to the junior prom or any prom. But she was sixteen years old and Diane felt strongly that Lisa should not be denied the experience of a prom; that she ought to be able to say that she went. Diane had gone to both her own junior and senior proms and regarded the earlier one, in particular, as something that should not be missed. There was much she tried to do to help Lisa with her personal relationships; there was more that she was powerless to do anything about. But perhaps the junior prom was within the limits of possibility.

"I thought about it a long time," Diane said, "long before Lisa ever got to be a junior. In fact, I think she may have been only a freshman when I started to think about her junior prom. I didn't want her to miss anything. When she didn't go to her senior prom, she'd know she didn't miss anything. I just thought she should go."

It was not something she discussed immediately with Lisa. Before any such discussion were held, Diane would have to resolve the question of who would take her. Diane thought about a suitable escort for almost two years and discovered the enormous advantage that comes from being part of a large family in which the children represent an enormous age spread.

Arlene's son, Carl, was Lisa's nephew, but he was a year older than Lisa and a senior in another school system. Carl was a very presentable young man who knew virtually nobody in Lisa's school. Before asking him, though, Diane had to talk it out with Arlene.

"Arlene didn't seem to care that much," Diane said. "She never thought proms were a big deal. She didn't go to her own prom and she was never sorry she didn't go." But Arlene had no objection to Carl taking Lisa, and the more she thought about it the more she came to agree with Diane that it might be a nice experience for Lisa.

As for Carl, he shared fully in his family's caring about Lisa but when he was asked if he would take her, he hesitated; he was frightened.

"I was afraid," he said, "afraid of people saying things to Lisa. When they say things, I get upset, I start to scream and yell and throw punches. I think it upsets me more than it does her. Once, long before the junior prom came up, I took Lisa out to pick up a pizza that Grandma had ordered. We were in the pizza parlor and I told them what I wanted and the counterman asked Lisa what she wanted and I said that she was with me. Then a couple of kids just outside the door started to laugh. Kids about my age. I went off. I felt really bad. I went outside, yelling and cursing, and I took the pizza one kid was eating out of his hand and I pushed it into his face. I started throwing people around. I was screaming at the top of my lungs and then somebody grabbed me and told me to calm down, that I could get locked up for what I was doing.

"So I stopped and I went back into the pizza parlor. Lisa said to me, 'You didn't have to do that,' and I told her, 'Yes, I did.'"

Carl asked his mother if the family would regard him as a "rat" if he declined to take Lisa to the prom.

"No, they won't think that," Arlene told him. "You'll only do it if you want to do it." It occurred to Arlene then, and later, that his source of concern—his fear that somebody would say something to Lisa and that he would explode in rage and violence again—was not a concern that she or most women she knew would have. Most women would ignore the insult so as not to make Lisa feel worse, she thought. But man cannot accept abuse as can woman.

Finally, Carl agreed. But would Lisa?

Lisa recalls now that she was not eager to go but she did agree and for a while, at least, she seemed to be caught up in the junior prom mystique.

"I remember that she was all thrilled and excited about it," Arlene said. "It took a lot of courage to do what she did and she took it all very well, keeping a big smile on her face. I admired her for that." She was also very proud of her son. She could not have told him how much; Carl was not the sort of boy who liked to hear that sort of talk.

Still, there were things she had to say to him. "I told him that if he couldn't do it nicely, then he shouldn't do it at all. When the time came, he was nice. He was all smiles, and if he still had reservations about what might happen, he didn't inflict them on anybody."

Carl and Lisa agreed to go about two months before the prom was held. That gave Diane time to make Lisa a gown. She shopped quickly but carefully. She wanted everything to be just right. She found a pattern she liked at a little shop at Great Valley. The pattern described a sort of a peasant gown with a scoop neck and long sleeves. She hunted further and found some off-white satin at a very good price and some purple ribbon for the neck in King of Prussia. And then with great care, she started to sew.

"I'm slow as sap," she said. "I had to leave two months just to make sure that it was done right."

The prom was held in the banquet room of a Holiday Inn on April 22, 1978 at 8 o'clock. It was a mild spring evening, so mild that Lisa didn't even bother to wear a coat over the gown that Diane had made. Jennifer did her hair, which looked very nice; but she was wearing a pair of new white shoes that were too tight. That was a bother; when she bought them, they seemed to fit quite well.

Carl wore his best dress-up suit, a three-piece gabardine, with a striped shirt, open at the collar. He arrived early at Lisa's with his parents. Much of the family was assembled there—even Anna, Mary's mother, was there, although she was then quite old and ailing. But she came and they had a pleasant time talking as Diane took snapshots with a flash attachment in Lisa's living room. They remain among Diane's most treasured possessions. In one of them, Carl can be seen affixing a corsage of pink carnations to Lisa's left wrist.

"He had ordered a spring bouquet," Diane recalled. "That's what she wanted. But when the flowers came they were carnations. I was furious. I tried to take them back, but by the time I got there the florist was closed."

Nevertheless it was a most pleasant moment, and before long Lisa and Carl were out their front door. They showed up promptly at eight and the ballroom was almost empty. But it was nicely decorated with little lights on the walls. There was plenty of food—meatballs in tangy sauce, cocktail franks, egg rolls, fried shrimp, cheese and crackers, chips and dip, soda and dinner mints. There was also a pretty good band playing, imported all the way from south-central New Jersey.

Her classmates had given the prom a name—"Pieces of April"—and each couple was given a small souvenir program. In it was some verse written by one of Lisa's classmates, an effort to give the juniors something to remember their prom, that period of special sweetness in their lives.

> Looking back
> why is it
> I only remember the happy times?
> Times which have
> slipped by silently.
> If
> I had realized
> would things be different?
> It is past.
> Now,
> I am alone
> with only
> my memories.

Carl escorted Lisa through the semidarkness to their place.

"We got a table," Carl said, "a big table, with eight or ten chairs around us. People began to arrive and nobody sat down with us. We sat there for a long time and I started getting pissed off. Finally, somebody Lisa was friends with in school came over and we were talking and he said 'Who's your date?' She just said, 'This is Carl.' We didn't tell anybody that I was her nephew. There wasn't any point in doing that. After that, a couple of other couples sat down with us. But as I remember it, all the other tables were filled except ours. It was O.K. We slow danced a couple of times. I'm not much of a dancer. We stayed there a couple of hours. To tell you the truth, I don't think we stayed for the whole thing. Nobody made any comments, except somebody said they thought she looked nice. Something like that. She did look nice. We walked back out to the car and I remember thinking that I was glad it had gone O.K. I mean, I didn't really want to get into a fight but I think I would have if somebody had said something nasty. And then I would have ruined it for her."

The next Monday, back in school, some of Lisa's classmates

talked among themselves in little groups in the hall. Some snickered; some noted that she had a very good-looking escort. Lisa agreed with them about her escort. But neither the prom nor her junior year has become a beautiful memory for her. Her classmate's poem never was her poem.

For all of her early indifference to it, Arlene now tends to think that the prom may have been a good thing for Lisa. The family showed, once again, that it cared. And in her view, both Lisa and Carl demonstrated courage in attending the dance and comporting themselves as they did. Diane, who so wanted it to be a beautiful moment for Lisa, has no regrets, either.

"She went and she experienced it. She saw what it was all about. I always told Lisa to go for the big brass ring, that was always my philosophy for her. Go for it, just like everybody else."

Chapter Ten

James Katowitz was accustomed to being both competitive and successful. As a bear of an undergraduate at Haverford College in the late 1950s, he was a formidable wrestler, an agile soccer player (especially for a man his size), and a discus thrower of considerable power. His classmates respected his abilities as a competitive broad jumper, too. And because he had good hands, the sort that sportscasters like to call soft hands when they occur among professionals, he was a fine tight end, at least in the modest sub-Ivy competition that the academically serious Quaker institution permitted itself. Haverford's academic traditions were dear to Katowitz, a psychology major, who won a fellowship and came to the University of Pennsylvania to study medicine, which he did with distinction. Actually, he almost didn't study medicine. He had a fine baritone voice, loved music, especially Bach, and might have become a professional singer. His music was a source of great satisfaction to him.

But in 1963, when he was a young resident working under Harold Scheie and examined Lisa for the first time, all he experienced was an uncommon sense of frustration and loss. Lisa was losing her face. She was losing her eyesight. There was nothing Katowitz could do about it. Like every doctor who had ever met or would ever meet Lisa, he was struck with her balance, her openness and her economically expressed sense of humor. He never forgot her, and over the years, as he honed his skills as a surgeon, he wondered if his particular specialty, a mating of ophthalmology and plastic surgery, would ever reach the point where it would do Lisa any good.

Suddenly, he seemed to be given an opportunity to help Lisa, but surely not in the way he had originally dreamed of doing. He and Whitaker had worked together with some frequency in a team assembled by Whitaker to do complicated craniofacial surgery. In the summer of 1981, Whitaker told him that he was calling the team together again to perform surgery on an especially severe case of neurofibromatosis. Katowitz then found himself confronting Lisa once again, although decidedly not under the circumstances he had hoped medical technology would yield when he first saw her. He had not really looked at her closely for years and the devastation of the face of the child he so admired was hurtful, even for a sensitive man who had tried so assiduously to inure himself to surrendering his emotions to such sadness.

It seemed to Whitaker that her left eye was probably not worth saving but that was outside his province and he asked Katowitz about it. The eye was badly impaired by the years of persistent glaucoma, heightened pressure that had damaged the retina and optic nerve, despite the efforts of doctors to control it. The left eye was beset by cataracts as well. Cataracts are essentially opacities that glaze across the lens, and when they occur in young people, people in Lisa's age group, they are usually caused by an injury to the eye. Katowitz had treated young prize fighters for cataracts. In older people, doctors regarded cataracts as part of the aging process. In Lisa, it was impossible to say for sure what had caused them but Katowitz was mindful that the multiple surgical procedures necessary to relieve or control her glaucoma represented contributory insults to the eye. There had been no alternative to those procedures; the glaucoma pressure had to be brought down. But benefits derived from controlling the pressure had their price too.

In the eighteen years since Katowitz had first examined her,

123

Lisa's left eye had greatly enlarged to more than three times normal size. And so the surgeon who had shared in Scheie's frustration in not being able to help her decisively and permanently when she was a baby was now considering the removal of an eye—for mostly aesthetic reasons.

He looked at the face he had first seen so long ago. The extent of the growth of tumor had been cruel and awesome. But Katowitz had to make sure that Whitaker was right, that the left eye really was beyond saving.

He sat before her, covered her right eye and started with the simplest of tests.

"Can you see out of the left eye? Can you see my hand?" His hand was a couple of feet from her face.

"No, not really."

He wiggled his fingers close to her face.

"Can you see my fingers at all?"

"No."

The test was slow and deliberate. He tried light and color. Her left eye could detect some light but no color at all, not even a bright red. Then he tried more sophisticated tests, including taking a picture of the inside of her eye with an ultrasound machine. None of it looked especially promising. He checked pressure in both of her eyes with a pneumatonometer. In millimeters of mercury, pressure was about 35 in her right eye and 30 in her left. Normal was closer to 21 millimeters of mercury.

Lisa wanted a more normal face. But was it worth having an eye removed? Katowitz was not sure what to tell her.

"You want a decision before the eighth of December, don't you?" she asked him.

"Yes," Katowitz said, "absolutely." He let his mind wander to real and unreal options, talking half to her, half to himself.

"If we could only find a way to reduce the size of the orbit . . . then perhaps we could fit you with a contact lens over the eye. . . . But it is not likely that we could achieve anything. . . . You know, it's easy for me to say that if it were me,

I'd do it. But I'm not you. We have to respect what you want. But it is a concern to me that you would go through so much and have that detract very significantly from your whole appearance, which is what you are striving for."

He continued his examination and expressed his concern about the cataracts.

"Can't you shatter cataracts?" she asked him.

He was noncommittal. "There are different techniques."

The two were alone in the examining room, except for me. Verna Mitros waited outside. It was one of the longest days of her life, the afternoon of November 24, 1981, the day that Whitaker first broached the idea to Lisa of removal of her left eye, the day when the last major physical evaluations would be made in preparation for major surgery. Verna had heard quite enough that morning; she saw no reason to listen to Katowitz as she had to Whitaker.

"It will not be just a matter of taking out masses," he said. "The shape and contour of your face will be distorted. Your eyelid openings will have to be reduced."

"Yes, Dr. Whitaker told me that," Lisa said.

"There are several ways we can approach that but what we have discussed is to try to reduce the length of the openings. I'm sure that Dr. Whitaker has pointed out to you that we will be removing most of the muscles and nerve here, so that this means you won't be able to close your eye in the same way. So we have got to protect it.

"The most important thing for us is to maintain the integrity and the function of your right eye. It sounds like a paradox but we are very much concerned about protecting what you do have. This means that as we are doing the surgery, we are going to have to make some decisions about how we protect your eye.

"Most young people can adjust to exposure of the eye. If we carefully nurture the epithelium, the covering of the eye, for periods of time, the eye adjusts. We have cases where the eye really doesn't need to close. . . ."

As she had with Whitaker, Lisa remained silent, almost as if she were back in her college classroom, listening to a lecture.

"So, let me just summarize," Katowitz said. "We are not proposing to do anything to your right eye. What happens on the left side is up to you. As far as the left side is concerned, you have a cataract, you have poor function, you probably would never get a good result with the eye. I don't think you'd ever be able to read with it. So if we take that into account and look at you as a person in a whole way, we are suggesting the possibility of removal of the eye, but it is your decision.

"If you decide to leave the left eye in, I am not saying there won't be any improvement in the way you look. I am not saying that. There will be some improvement because we are going to do a lot of things. But the left eye is almost three times the size of a normal eye and there are only limited things that we can do to camouflage it. Do you have any questions?"

"I want to think about all of this," she said, looking downward toward the floor.

"Well, when you go home and you think of questions, write them down on a piece of paper and call me. We'll talk about it together on the telephone. Our plan as of now is to stay away from your right eye; we want to preserve what you have there. In terms of making your lids look better, I'd prefer a staged approach. We won't try to do too much at once. I know that what I've told you is a lot for you to digest."

"I guess it is."

"Oh, the tear drainage system," Katowitz said, remembering to go into a possible consequence of surgery. He wanted to make sure that she knew as much as possible while she was making up her mind in the next few days. "Work may be done there, too. We might have a tearing problem in all of this, but I will take care of that later. Droopy eyelids and tearing, if that's a problem, will have to wait till later. Until we finish all the big things. We have only a certain number of opportunities to do it well and so the major things have to come first."

"If I let you take the left eye out, what will you put in its place?" she asked.

"Well, we would probably take a piece of tissue from inside of your leg. We would take out a circle of skin. We would take the skin and the fat underneath. We could put that in your left eye instead of a plastic ball, sew muscles to it and then it will move. Then, over that, we could put a plastic shell to match up with your other eye. It will add some motion to your eye. But it will never have complete motion.

"I've known you since you were four and I think you're just a wonderful person. You haven't changed. I think it is wonderful where we've come to a point in time where we can be of more help to you. You're a sweet child and it is good to be able to offer you something. Not everything we'd like, but something."

"I want to think about it."

"Yes. Think about it and call me."

We rose to leave and Lisa looked at me. "You know, I have to get my phonograph fixed. I haven't been able to listen to any music."

I asked her how she felt about Katowitz's presentation.

"I want to think about it."

Chapter Eleven

~~~~~

The night before the event that Whitaker had planned as carefully as he could, as audaciously as he dared, the surgery clearly containing the potential both for giving Lisa a new face and for claiming her life, he and other doctors and all manner of nurses and technicians filed in and out of Lisa's private room. They took meticulous notes and collected data, bravely assuring a weary and fearful family that all would be well.

One physician made two such visits. She was Dr. Ellen Jantzen, who was trained as an anesthesiologist but who also possessed the grace and the instincts of the old-fashioned general practitioner, embracing the compassion of another age, seemingly so long ago and far away. Her first visit to Lisa's room lasted about forty-five minutes; the other about fifteen.

Jantzen, educated not so long before at Mount Holyoke and Harvard Medical School, considered herself a conservative woman; she stubbornly tried to conserve the high standards of professionalism she had so recently been taught. She always tried to see her patients twice on the night before they were to undergo major surgery. She regarded the first conversation as a chance to get as much information as she could about their general health, so that she could make a critical assessment as to whether the patient's physical condition at the moment indicated that he or she was, in fact, fit enough to have surgery.

Once Jantzen determined this, she'd tell the patient what to expect the next morning.

Then she'd come back a second time to see if any questions had occurred to the patient, questions that might have been forgotten in the bravado nervousness and cold dread universally shared by anyone who has ever entrusted his life to a surgeon.

On this particular night, Jantzen encountered two distinct and separate Lisas. In the first meeting, with Mary and Diane present, Lisa seemed intent on putting any apprehensions they might have had to rest. And so she likened her surgery to an episode of a nighttime soap opera that she and Mary frequently watched.

"When you wake up," Jantzen told her, "you'll have an endotracheal tube in your throat. It's nothing to be concerned about; we have to do it because there will be swelling and we have to keep your breathing passages clear."

"How many inches wide will it be?" Lisa asked.

"Only about half an inch."

"That's nothing. On *Flamingo Road* they showed one of those tubes not too long ago and it was much bigger. It was gigantic. Half an inch is nothing." They all laughed.

Jantzen then listened to Lisa's heart and lungs. Both sounded fine. Her thyroid gland felt a little large, Jantzen thought, and for a time she wondered if Lisa would actually be deemed operable. But when the tests came back, they showed thyroid function within normal limits.

Two hours later, Jantzen returned. Mary and Diane had gone home and Lisa was alone in her room in the Silverstein Pavilion of the Hospital of the University of Pennsylvania. A hospital never really becomes quiet when everyone leaves. Only lonelier. Lisa could hear hospital silence; the occasional squeaky footsteps of a nurse in rubber-soled shoes, the barely audible shallow rattle of a cart pushed by her room, bearing its eventide burden of medicine to kill infection, lessen pain, banish sleeplessness, diminish worry. At this late hour, Jantzen found her patient quite different.

"I do have some concerns," Lisa said.

"What are they?"

"I am concerned about the way I'm going to feel when I'm on my way to the operating room. I don't like to lie on the stretcher and see the tops of the hospital doors go by. Don't ask me why I'm so concerned about a silly thing like that, but I am and it's been preying on my mind."

It wasn't silly at all but it was noteworthy. It had been ten years since the last surgery and she could still remember seeing the tops of the doors go by.

Jantzen took her hand. It was shaking slightly and it was decidedly clammy. She assured Lisa that she understood but promised that this time there'd be no discomfort of any kind on the way to the operating room. She'd see to that.

An hour or so after she left, Lisa called Mary one last time.

"I don't want you to worry about anything," she told her mother. "This operation was meant to be. I know it will be all right. I just know it."

"I know it, too," said Mary, who had been waiting for the call and who couldn't have even tried to sleep until she received it. "We've waited twenty-one years for this."

Jantzen kept her promise to Lisa. At 5:15 the next morning, Lisa received fifteen milligrams of Valium in pill form, followed by intramuscular injections of eight milligrams of morphine sulfate and three-tenths of a milligram of atropine, all of it ordered by the supervising anesthesiologist, Dr. John Lecky, after he had conferred with Jantzen.

When Lecky went to Lisa's room at 6:45 to personally bring her to the operating room, she was awake. But he could accurately report that he found her "comfortable but composed." The morphine and the Valium had woven so much gossamer around Lisa that for all she knew, she was going to the operating room not on a stretcher at all, but in Tom Selleck's Ferrari (she's a fan of his).

The atropine was not at all a part of the effort to tranquilize and sedate Lisa. Its use in this instance underscored the mystery that surrounds neurofibromatosis—a lack of knowledge so vast that a teaching hospital of the University of Pennsylvania's character takes no chances.

Atropine is an alkaloid derivative of belladonna, a plant also known as deadly nightshade. It is a poison that attacks the parasympathetic nervous system, the system that works without conscious control. In sufficient dose, it can subvert that system to kill a human. But given in minute amounts, as it has been with much safety since its discovery in 1833, atropine provides many services for the sick: it can dilate pupils for diagnostic purposes and it can even provide relief for gastrointestinal cramps. It has a particularly benign characteristic for the victims of neurofibromatosis who are about to undergo surgery. Neurofibromatosis can be accompanied by a relatively rare tumor called pheochromocytoma, which is capable of secreting excessive amounts of the hormones epinephrine and norepinephrine, which, in turn, can cause arrhythmias, irregular heartbeat, and blood pressure to climb rapidly to dangerous, sometimes lethal levels.

Lecky wasn't sure whether Lisa had a pheochromocytoma or not. As it turned out, she did not have one. But such tumors aren't outwardly visible. The presence of a pheochromocytoma was not indicated, since Lisa had no medical history of high blood pressure, nor the rapid onset of headaches nor acute anxiety.

That wasn't totally true. She *did* have acute anxieties. But all of hers had been caused by ordinary, visible people, not by rare and hidden tumors. But those kinds of anxieties went largely unreported in her medical records.

An elaborate urine analysis, done over a period of twenty-four hours, might have given doctors an indication as to whether there were excessive amounts of either epinephrine or norepinephrine in Lisa. But it wasn't ordered, and even if it had been Lecky probably would have prescribed the atropine anyhow. He wanted to be very certain that there were no noxious reflexes under anesthesia, bad surprises that could compromise her respiration, and her chances of survival, while she was undergoing surgery.

It was just before seven o'clock and Lisa's stretcher was finally in the gray-beige tile operating room, gliding across a floor of tiny black, blue and white swirls, a floor that seemed to defy anyone who would try to say what color it really was. There was hardly anyone there as Lecky and Jantzen started their work, setting up an arterial line to monitor blood gases and pressure in her arteries, the vessels that carry blood away from the heart to the rest of the body; a venous line to monitor pressure in the venous system, the system that carries the blood back to the heart that pumps it.

Others began to file in. People in clean, wrinkled, olive-fronted green frocks and light blue surgical masks. The murmuring rose. Lecky noted Lisa's arterial blood pressure was 100/60, which was quite normal for her.

Joyce Carr, one of Whitaker's favorite scrub nurses, was an early arrival. She had been a nurse for only two years, ever since her graduation from Villanova, and had come to the Hospital of the University of Pennsylvania because she wanted to work in the intensive care nursery.

But when she visited the hospital for an interview, accompanied by another candidate for a nursing job, the other young woman said she wanted to tour the operating room.

"All right," Carr said, "I'll go with you," even though it was the nursery she wanted to see. But when she entered the operating room, she changed her mind.

"I took one look at it," she told me, "and I decided this is where I want to work."

Some of her friends, including some in nursing, wondered what she saw in it. There was no financial incentive to be an operating room nurse, unless she were "on call," for emergency weekend work, for which the hospital paid her a dollar an hour.

"You can see," she said, "that we don't do it for the money. Sometimes, when I talk to my nursing friends, we compare notes on what we do and they say, 'My God, how can you do *that?'* The sight of blood scares them. I suppose that every nurse in the OR has felt uncomfortable with one procedure or another, but at one point you get used to it and then it's really your job."

She and Whitaker worked well together. She admired his constant striving for perfection; he respected her caring so much about his patients, all the patients, it seemed, even though she sometimes assisted in as many as four different operations in a single day.

Carr walked over to Jantzen. She hadn't met Lisa yet but she had heard about her and the extraordinary surgery she had elected. She wondered what sort of person would willingly accept that sort of punishment.

"What's she like?" Carr asked.

"She hasn't looked at herself in a mirror for a year," Jantzen said.

Carr could not conceive of anyone with a face so unacceptable that she could not look at herself.

Slowly, she approached the stretcher. She very much wanted to reassure Lisa, say something, anything that would make her feel better about what she was to go through, if not about herself. Lisa was still awake. But she was drowsy, her mind as much in phantasm as in reality now.

"Hello," Carr said. "I want to check your i.d. band."

"Hello," Lisa said.

"She is my age," Carr thought. "She's about my size. How many days do we spend just looking at ourselves and each other? How vain I am."

There was no conversation. There did not need to be, even if Lisa had not been sleepy. Over a period of years, Lisa had come to regard anyone who said anything at all of a nonhostile or nonpatronizing nature as somebody who might want to be a friend. Carr checked the identification band and walked back to her table and dutifully began to assemble the dull stainless steel equipment that would alter forever the face of the young woman she had just seen: five scalpels for cutting; a row of hemostats to clamp blood vessels that would be cut by the scalpels; a row of scissors; a row of spoon-shaped elevators, little contraptions that surgeons would use to lift up tissue; retractors to pull back flesh so that surgeons could see their objectives more clearly; bone benders and bone cutters. All of them had been previously steamed and sterilized at high temperatures in an autoclave, a kind of little oven in the operating room, then laid out on sterile linen, waiting.

They moved Lisa onto the operating table. "Is there anything I can do to help?" Lisa asked, as she was placed on it. There was nothing she could do. She had already done it.

"Just relax," Jantzen said. "You're going to sleep, now, you're going to get very sleepy."

They gave her a minuscule dose of curare, another poison-become-muscle relaxant, and 100 milligrams of succinylcholine chloride, which also relaxes muscles. Then they gave her 250 milligrams of pentobarbitol, a barbiturate that induces sleep. Lisa was asleep by 7:30, less than forty-five seconds after pentobarbitol was injected. Because they had given her the muscle relaxants, it was that much easier to achieve what the doctors called intubation, the insertion of the oropharnyngeal airway into her mouth. It was done easily; there were no adverse reflexes. She would have to breathe by mouth, because after surgery actually began, her nasal passages would become swollen from the trauma of cutting. In the hours to come, there would be much cutting.

Then the anesthesia machine took over, giving her a mix of nitrous oxide and enflurane that would be monitored closely but easily and with accuracy by Lecky and Jantzen, who sat behind their equipment beyond the side of the operating table.

Her breathing sounds as monitored by the anesthesiologists were equal on both sides of her chest, which meant the tube went where it was supposed to.

After sleep set in, firmly, deeply, Lisa's head was shaved. She was shaved first with hair clippers, then with a straight razor. The shaving had not been done the night before to minimize the chances of an infection setting in from the nick of a razor. Then she was brushed with an iodine solution called Pharmadine, an effective sterilizing agent. It was poured on gauze and rubbed over her entire body by members of the surgical team.

As all this was going on, Whitaker, Katowitz and Dr. Donato LaRossa stood by, trying to make the initial decisions that would determine the course of surgery. LaRossa's specialty was microsurgery and he was there at Whitaker's invitation. Normally, he was involved in that aspect of plastic surgery that handles severe cases of injury, when tissue has to be moved around. Examples are cases of severed fingers or toes that have to be reimplanted.

But Whitaker felt that once this particular surgery got underway, he might very well need the expertise of LaRossa. The microsurgeon had attempted to prepare himself for the surgery by meeting with Lisa on November 24, the same day that she had met with Whitaker and Katowitz for the last major physical evaluation before surgery.

LaRossa had come into Examining Room No. 9 to make his own evaluation after Whitaker was finished. He had personal reservations about what sort of contribution he might be able to make to such a surgery, but none of his concerns showed as he stood before Lisa and spoke to her carefully and quietly. He was gentle but direct.

"My role in this is to provide some additional skin cover where Dr. Whitaker has to remove tissue. I want to tell you some of the possible places where we can get this tissue from. I want to get your reaction to that. I want to do it because what I do will leave more scars than what Dr. Whitaker does. But the scars will be in areas where you can cover them with clothing."

"Scars don't bother me, doctor," she said.

He then explained to her that a problem was to get tissue of the proper thickness. Tissue to be used on the face has to be relatively thin and LaRossa basically had two options: one, to take some skin from near the face—the shoulder, for example— bring it to the face, plant part of it there, but leave the other end of it temporarily attached to where it came from, to assure an adequate blood supply. After it "took" on her face, it would be divided from its source.

"I'm not too clear on what you mean by that," she said.

LaRossa rang for a hand towel, and when it arrived showed her how they might do such a procedure, stretching the cloth from his face to his arm. If done, it would mean that Lisa's arm would be kept immobile near her face for a time. That sort of tissue transfer is called a flap, as opposed to a graft.

"That's amazing," she said.

"Of course, we can also get tissue from your foot and connect it to your face with a microvascular procedure, connecting the small blood vessels. Do you follow me?"

"Yes," she said, barely audible.

"But it's usually better if we can use tissue that's local," he continued. "It's a lot simpler, it's a little more reliable and the color is better. The closer you are to your face, the more likely it is that the color is going to be the same." He explained that skin pigment intensifies as it moves from the face toward the feet. Matching facial skin is easier if the tissue is taken from close to the face.

"I still don't understand how a skin graft stays in place."

"A graft, if that is what we do, is a thin shaving of skin, taken with a machine from another part of your body in the operating room. If we put it in another spot, it will receive blood and it will grow. It is sort of like planting something."

"But how is it attached, how does it stay on?"

"You just lay it on there and the blood vessels grow into it," he said. "And after four or five days, it takes."

LaRossa told her there was a possibility that she wouldn't need elaborate microsurgery.

"It is just possible that the tissue rearrangement may work out so that all the areas we want will be covered and we won't have to borrow any tissue from anywhere else, except for those ribs."

"Do you have any idea how long surgery will take?"

"Six to ten hours, I would guess."

"Six to ten hours," she whispered. "That's a long time. I don't care, you know. I was just curious."

"Yes," LaRossa said. "I know."

Lisa asked him how long she'd have to stay in the hospital after surgery.

"Hard to say. It might be two weeks. Two and a half weeks."

"What are the odds of my getting out before Christmas?"

"I'd say the chances are pretty good."

That conversation had occurred two weeks ago. Lisa went to sleep under the impression that there might very well be all manner of flaps and grafts done during surgery. But now, as LaRossa, Whitaker and Katowitz talked about what they ought to do and how they ought to do it, they remained uncertain as to how much microsurgery might be needed. LaRossa, taking no chances, had marked her arms and shoulders as sources for flaps and the top of one foot as the possible site where a graft might be taken. As the surgeons gathered around Lisa and studied her face, they tried to assess just how much usable skin might be left after the tumors were removed.

Whitaker looked at Lisa's face. "I'm trying to decide," he said, "where the best locations for incisions would be."

On an illuminated screen twelve or fifteen feet behind him were Lisa's x-rays, as well as photocopies of pictures that Whitaker had marked up in advance, as sort of a strategy for surgery. But like a general preparing to commit his troops to a battle in which they would be outnumbered, Whitaker was prepared to alter strategy at any time.

Katowitz looked at the pictures and the enormity of the problem.

"It is like looking at a piece of Carrara marble," Katowitz said. "There is a *David* in there somewhere, if only we have the skill to find it."

Looking at Lisa's x-rays did not make Whitaker think of Carrara, or of any aesthetic or medical judgments that were even remotely Michelangelican in nature.

A large deformity in the left side of her head clearly showed. It was a mass of bone, laden with cysts, that had been attacked by neurofibromas. Her maxillary sinuses were filled with tumor. Her left frontal sinus was partially obliterated with tumor and there seemed to be some in the right sinus as well.

The bony orbits, or cavities, that held her eyes were not normally developed. On both the left and right sides, there seemed to be bone lacking toward the back of the orbit. Her cheekbones were also irregular. Her left eye was enormous, bloated by years of glaucoma. The right eye, where doctors had been more successful over the years in keeping pressures down, looked much better.

"Obviously, the big task in the future will be to maintain the right eye," Katowitz said, as they stood before the screen, studying the x-rays.

At 8:44, Whitaker sutured both her eyes shut so that they could not be accidentally injured by a scalpel while the removal of tumors took place. Three minutes later, he sutured some toweling to the back of her scalp, which, in turn, was sutured to other toweling. Her body, covered with sterile linen, was indeed an island of sterility and the suturing of yet more linen to her scalp was an effort to maintain the sterility that existed in the middle of the room.

Looking at her x-rays, her photographs and her face as it lay below and slightly in front of him, Whitaker slowly began to paint his surgical targets with a marker dipped in methylene blue dye. Actual surgery did not begin until 9:03, and the surgeon to cut first was not Whitaker. It was Dr. James E. Zins, chief resident in plastic surgery, who had the task of harvesting bone and cartilage from Lisa's ribs on the right side. Whitaker, Katowitz and LaRossa continued discussing what might be removed as Whitaker continued to apply the blue dye with a marker. I was curious as to precisely what Zins had to do to remove rib bone, but there was no way I could get close to him and continue listening to Whitaker, Katowitz and LaRossa. I stayed put.

There was an orientation problem maddening to a layman, but not bothersome to Whitaker and experienced surgeons. In one instant, Whitaker was getting an upside-down view of a face upon which gravity had its usual effect—the tumors tended to sink inward and sideways and not be nearly so conspicuous as they were in the photographs that were on the wall behind him, photographs taken of her not when she was lying down, but when she was seated.

"I'd like to remove all of this," Whitaker said, pointing to a mass of tumor on her face.

"You know, there's good tissue here on the right side, under the tumor," Katowitz said.

"So I see."

Lisa had wanted her eyebrows thinned down and Katowitz and Whitaker discussed how much eyebrow tissue they would be able to excise.

"We won't really know until we get in there," Whitaker said. "More blue, please." A nurse poured more of it into a little container on a table within the operational island. Where there was cross-hatching, it meant they would try to remove the tumor from underneath, leaving skin that would be stretched to cover areas where both skin and tumor would be taken.

At 9:17, Whitaker began to inject her face and the tumors on it with a mixture of lidocaine, a local anesthetic, and epinephrine, the very same sympathomimetic substance Lecky and Jantzen had ascertained she would not produce too much of herself.

But at this point, they were seeking some constriction of the blood vessels. Whitaker was trying to minimize the blood loss that would start the moment he cut into a tumor. The constriction that reduces bleeding also causes blood pressure to rise. From her perch behind the operating table, Jantzen increased the amount of enflurane and also gave Lisa a ganglionic blocker through the same venous line, which decreased activity in nerve cell bodies, to minimize the chance of arrythmia. Blood pressure eased again.

Whitaker measured various grotesque elements on Lisa's face, calling the measurements out to a nurse.

"Right horizontal palpebral fissure, 44 millimeters; left horizontal palpebral fissure, 44 millimeters; lateral nasal width, 66 millimeters, right eyebrow width, 80 millimeters. . . ." The nurse took down the measurements quickly.

Then, at 9:30, two hours after Lisa had gone to sleep, the planning was over. Whitaker put down his marker, picked up a scalpel and made his first incision.

Chapter Twelve

The initial incision stripped away an enormous mass of tumor. Was it surgery or sorcery? It did, after all, seem as though Lisa had been under a mask of wax but it took the scalpel to truly reveal the enemy—the neurofibromas themselves, the tangible evidence of the genetic mistake.

They were uncovered as a tangle of thin, ugly, wormlike things underneath what had appeared to be one enormous tumor on the surface. Their consistency was not unlike that of rubber. Whitaker snipped at them, tugged at them with his scissors and quickly, deftly, removed dozens, scores of them. It took fully five minutes before he felt that he was finished with the first incision. Across the table, Zins, assisted by nurse Joan Widua, continued to slowly work his way toward the rib and cartilage that Whitaker would need later in the operation.

"I'm glad to see some normal tissue," Whitaker said, as he continued to work on the left side of her head. And then, after one move of the scalpel, he told the doctors gathered around him, "We have just cut and paralyzed her forehead permanently." He had known that this would happen and so had Lisa. She accepted that as part of the price.

It was not totally silent in the operating room. There was a quiet, a certain respectable murmur.

A year before this I had attended open-heart surgery at the

University of Alabama in Birmingham. On that occasion, the room was whisper quiet. But quiet comes with order, and order in open-heart surgery is derived from the clarity of the problem presented by a triple by-pass and the technology developed to deal with it. Heart surgery was conducted mostly in silence, eyes peering over masks and other eyes receiving messages with no words needed, the way members of a small chamber orchestra can gain a sense of each other with practice and establish their own dynamics, their own *tempi*, without a conductor. But with Lisa's operation, there was no music, no heart-lung machine to impose form from its own whispering. There never was a machine that could have dealt with the chaos of so much tumor and without such a machine, precise planning was impossible. It was quite impossible to say, in advance, much of anything about what would happen once the cutting began. And so of necessity, the words were saved and there was talk during surgery. If order could not be planned in advance, perhaps the awesome disorder presented by the neurofibromatosis could be discussed, clearly and clinically, right then and there.

There had not seemed to be very much bleeding from the removal of the first tumor. Jantzen, watching from her post just outside and behind the island of sterile linen, noted in her log just after the incision was completed that Lisa's blood looked healthy and well oxygenated. Neither she nor Lecky, who was next to her, saw any need to administer a unit of blood. Not then.

At 9:37, Whitaker snipped pieces of neurofibromas away from her left eyelid. At 9:40, the blood vessels that had been exposed from the first excision were being cauterized to stop the bleeding. I could not see who was doing the cauterizing because his back was to me, but in what was a portent of the dread that was to come, the tissue did not seem to respond to the process. The hot cautery touched the blood vessels properly enough, but they continued to leak as though nothing had been done.

Zins kept working on the right rib and Whitaker and Katowitz found more salvageable tissue in her scalp than they had thought.

Two minutes later, Whitaker was "debulking" her left temporal region—removing neurofibromas from under the temple and saving whatever good skin there was over it. By 9:48, he had found much evidence of neurofibromatosis in the area around her cheek and was removing it. At that point, she had lost 200 cubic centimeters of blood but Lecky and Jantzen had begun no transfusion as yet. They were replacing the volume of fluid lost, however, with a mixture of dextrose and water, as well as albumin, a simple but absolutely vital protein that enables the body to carry on osmosis (the process that maintains our fluids in proper balance). If they had permitted her albumin to drop too low, there would have been risk of an overaccumulation of fluid in the body, a perilous condition that doctors call edema.

According to Jantzen's records, Lisa got her first pint, called a "unit" of blood, at 9:50. Her body held about five quarts of blood. It had been decided to begin transfusions once she lost more than two pints.

Things seemed to be happening very quickly. For a few brief moments, it seemed as if it might turn out to be a short day after all. There seemed a chance that a surgery so awesome to contemplate might slip by uneventfully. Shortly before ten o'clock, Whitaker, who had been removing neurofibromas up and down the left side of her face, said he thought that the lower part of her face would retain nerve function and thus expression. To Lisa, that would be a precious gift. He also exposed the cartilage of her left ear and brought it to a more vertical position. Cauterization was started there, too, with the same result.

"We've got the diseased tissue out of her cheekbone and we'll decide how to rebuild it later," Whitaker said. As doctors worked, they clearly left many options until later and as the list of things left hanging became longer and longer, it became clearer and clearer that there never had been a chance for a short day.

Even though decisions were left unmade, there was a rhythm to it all, but a decidedly different one than that offered by open-heart surgery. Here it was cut, cauterize and suture, then move on quickly to the next surgical objective to cut, cauterize and suture again. There was rhythm, but a strange one and nothing to derive reassurance from. Moves to new surgical objectives had to be ordered before the suturing and cauterization were completed in old objectives. The surgeons moved like aggressive generals, creating new fronts before old ones had really been conquered. There seemed little alternative; time would not permit waiting for each phase to be finished before a new phase began. The bleeding continued, as had been expected, and worst of all, the cauterization continued not to work even remotely the way it should have. A doctor in front of me kept applying the cautery, but when the cautery seared tissue, the tissue did not contract; the blood vessels, which have a muscle in them that normally reacts sharply to the cautery's burn, did not seem to react at all. The cautery was applied again and again. But the vessels that had been infiltrated and changed by the neurofibromatosis would not shrink down the way they do in most other patients, patients with ordinary flesh. There was nothing to do but to keep trying. But what would happen if the blood vessels never responded? It was impossible not to consider the possibility.

She had wanted this so badly. "You can't understand how it is," she had told me. "You haven't been there."

Ivory hands worked under sterile gloves, limber, rubber-gloved hands, gloves pulled above the cuffs of their surgical gowns, now splattered with amber and red. The hands were all any observer could see, now. Hands, cautery and tissue—tissue that would not stop bleeding.

"Her tissues aren't responding very well," Whitaker said as he removed more neurofibromas from under her scalp. "It's like wet Kleenex." The blood vessels continued to remain mostly open. And so, inevitably, the blood loss was beginning to accelerate.

Her prospects did not seem especially promising. But from Whitaker's point of view, it was unthinkable to consider stopping. She was young with a strong heart. He did not think her condition threatened her existence. He had promised her and he had promised himself that he would try a new approach. And so he tried, tried very hard to create a new face.

He was finding more usable skin that he thought could stay just where it was, and as he did it became less probable that LaRossa, who was standing by, would have to perform a substantial microsurgery.

LaRossa left sometime later, assured by Whitaker that no microsurgery would be needed.

At 10:20, Whitaker asked Katowitz to begin the removal of Lisa's left eye. In her final talk with Katowitz, she was frightened only at the enucleation process, not the prospect of losing residual vision. "That," Katowitz told me, "gives you an idea of how pathetic it has been for her."

Her face was now bleeding profusely, the transfusion of her third unit of blood began and Lecky, watching his instruments, gave his first oral advisory in a very clear voice: "We have an appreciable blood loss here."

The operating physicians, as much teachers as they were surgeons, described what they were doing and what they were finding. There were residents and interns and other physicians from the hospital coming into the room for relatively brief periods of time to watch the operating surgeons. It might succeed and it might fail but whatever happened, the effort to give Lisa a new face was also a chance for them to learn. "I'm going to try to preserve as much of the lining of the left eye as possible," Katowitz said, as he began the process of enucleation. "That will be important."

Meanwhile, Whitaker quickly moved to the right side of the skull, drew his scalpel across a point two-thirds of the way back, and rolled the skin forward, so that he could remove neurofibromas there.

Zins, who had been working hard at harvesting ribs and was near to completing his objective, looked over at him. "Doctor, do you want two ribs or three?"

"Two will do it," Whitaker said quickly. Zins provided them, placing them on a table near the foot of the operating table, and by 10:45, he had completed suturing the rib wound closed. His job was far from over, however. There was much cauterizing to do. Little freshets of blood now made their way to the floor. Perhaps 100 sponges had been used; the floor looked almost as if no sponges had been used.

Zins was not perturbed by what he saw around him. He told himself that his colleagues were in control of the situation.

As cauteries were applied, Whitaker removed an enormous neurofibroma from the course of the superorbital nerve. Indeed, the tumor had actually become the nerve. The nerve had simply been absorbed by it and was no longer visible. The neurofibroma measured one and a half centimeters in diameter and it was six centimeters long. It looked like an enormous mass of insect larvae. If anybody wanted to contend that it was still a superorbital nerve, then it was ten to twenty times larger than a superorbital nerve ought to be. It was so gigantic that everyone in the room stopped what he or she was doing for a second to look at it. If there had been any doubt before, it was clear that this "plastic surgery" was hardly just that. At least, not if plastic surgery is delineated and defined by an effort to improve the looks of the patient. What was going on now was by no means purely aesthetic in nature. There were surely medical benefits that would accrue from the removal of so much diseased tissue from under her face and scalp.

Katowitz slowly cut through the muscles holding the left eye in its orbit. Derek Bruce, a neurosurgeon who was part of the team Whitaker had assembled, stood by Katowitz's side, assisting him in any way he could. "The trick is going to be to get this out without its contents rupturing," Katowitz said. It was just 10:50 when Katowitz successfully lifted Lisa's left eye out of its orbit. It was a sad victory. Again, everyone stopped what he or she was doing to look at it.

Lisa had always corrected family and friends if they called neurofibromatosis a disease.

"It's a disorder," she said, firmly. "A genetic disorder." But if she could have seen her own surgery, she might have agreed with them that disorder, while scientifically accurate, did not do justice to the power this thing had for destruction.

It had destroyed so much of her eye that even the professionals who had considerable experience with neurofibromatosis stared at it in wonderment. If it had been a normal eye, its sides would have been thick and white. But the sides of this eye were perilously thin, speckled with dark ominous spots where the wall of the eye had been much weakened by neurofibromatosis. It looked close to rupturing, bulging, as it did, with fluid and tumor. Katowitz placed it in a container of formalin so that he could study it later. In the orbit or "socket" behind the eye, Katowitz found still more tumor and began removing it. There seemed to be tumor everywhere. Scar tissue from previous surgeries and tumor, always tumor. Actually there were two kinds of tumor in the orbit. There were the neurofibromas themselves. And there was a glioma, which was a solid tumor.

"A big bag of worms," Katowitz muttered, half to himself.

At 11:04, Lecky said it again: "Appreciable blood loss here." By then he had given her eight units. Experienced surgeons and anesthesiologists know that in the course of a long and complicated surgery, a patient may lose fifteen pints, twenty pints, or even more. But there comes a point in all patients where the loss of blood cannot be compensated for. The reason is that repeated transfusions rob the blood of both its precious calcium and its fibrinogen.

Fibrinogen is a protein in the blood with a high molecular weight and gives blood its clotting factor. Clotting itself is simply the formation of a gelatinous substance at the ends of a blood vessel, causing the slowing or stopping of blood flow. It is the body's natural way of protecting itself when injury occurs. But with repeated transfusions over a relatively short period of time, the blood begins to lose its clotting factor. Different people have different tolerances for the transfusions that accompany surgery, but no human can go on taking endless transfusions in a short period of time. Lisa had not yet reached her limit, but there was apprehension that she soon would unless they could stop the bleeding.

Whitaker stopped what he was doing, stood away from the table and said firmly, his voice rising well above the murmuring, "Look, we have to stop the bleeding. Everyone should do whatever he can to stop the bleeding." Then, flatly and quietly to his scrub nurse: "These scissors aren't very good."

"Here you go," Carr replied, placing another pair firmly in his outstretched palm.

The surgical team was eager to comply with Whitaker's order. It was just that nobody knew how to do it.

At that point, William Jackson, a staff nurse, came into the operating room and told Katowitz that his office was calling for him. "One of your patients is having a problem and they want to know when you'll be through."

"Tell them tomorrow night," Katowitz sighed, looking at the work yet to be done. "No, tell them I'll try to call in an hour or so."

Katowitz then began to follow a plan he had that he hoped would improve Lisa's face. He had already been careful to preserve the rectus muscles that had made her left eye move. He took some skin and fat that had been removed from underneath the breast, shaped it to the volume of the eye he had just removed, and sewed it to the eye muscles.

"This becomes a living implant," he said, turning to me as he finished it. First a temporary, then a permanent prosthesis would soon go over that, which Katowitz hoped would move like a real eye. It was not exactly the way he had hoped he could help her all those years ago. Even now, if neurofibromatosis struck with equal fury at the eyes of another of his patients, there would be little he could do to stop it. Such is the power of the disease and the inadequacy of medicine to deal with it.

Katowitz was mindful that he had a most difficult problem with Lisa's eyes. Tumor had pulled the lids down toward the middle of her face. With the tumor gone, the lids could presumably be eased back to where they should have been in the first place. But the positioning of the lids on her face was not the major problem. On the left side, he had removed a vastly enlarged eye that would be replaced by a prosthesis of normal size. But on the right side, her real eye, somewhat outsized, would consequently look less attractive than the prosthesis. In an effort to make her face appear more symmetrical, he created two almond-shaped eye openings, by bringing the upper lid portion down and the lower one up, supported by a tendon that had been taken from her leg, a fascia lata. He reduced the size of her eyelids by one-half. And because both he and Whitaker agreed that after surgery there would be some sagging of the eyelids, he tilted them upward, overcorrecting them, so that when they did fall, they would be in the right place. Katowitz also saved the right eyelid's ability to blink. Blinking is controlled by the seventh cranial nerve and when he worked on that side of her face, he carefully avoided cutting it. On the left side, however, the nerve was destroyed in the course of surgery.

Jantzen started giving calcium intravenously after Lisa had lost ten pints of blood, shortly before noon, four and one-half hours after she went to sleep. The transfusions were going well; the cauterization efforts were not.

Lecky, who had repeatedly called the hospital's blood bank, noted that their attitude that morning was decidedly different than usual.

"They're usually defensive about their blood supply," he told me, "but today they're being very cooperative. They know who it's for."

Katowitz inserted some orange dye into her tearing system to see if it worked properly. "Her lacrimal systems are working," he said, so that all gathered around the operating table could hear.

At one point, Whitaker moved over to the foot of the operating table and began to fashion a new nose for Lisa out of the cartilage that Zins had taken from the rib. It was something she had very much wanted him to do, since the neurofibromatosis had destroyed her profile. He worked at fashioning the nose, looking up briefly every once in a while to see how the cauterization process was going. Some of the vessels had finally closed but she was still losing enormous amounts of blood. He started to think of things he could put off, compromises he might make. It could not go on indefinitely like this.

At 12:20, Whitaker made a critical discovery: Lisa's right eye was pulsating. And that meant the operation would have to be prolonged, even though blood losses were mounting.

It had not been noticed before, probably because she had so much tumor on her face that it eluded examinations. But now much of that tumor was gone. Clearly, the eye was picking up the pulsing of the brain, which moves in rhythm with the heart. It seemed reasonable to assume that somehow the dura, the lining around the brain, had intruded into the back of the eye socket. Normally, people have a bone between the temporal lobe of the brain and the back of the eye's orbit, which is called the sphenoid wing. It neatly keeps the brain where it is supposed to be. In Lisa, the bone was missing.

"That pulsing eye cannot be tolerated," Whitaker said to me. "It would be harmful to her right eye, might make it work itself out of its orbit and destroy her vision entirely." He then looked at Derek Bruce. "We need a craniotomy."

A *craniotomy*. The opening of the skull. This is surely a most disturbing procedure that surgical technology has given the rest of us to think about. For here, the surgeon's uncertain art hovers about the brain, the only organ that makes us special, if, indeed, anything does. It is unforgiving surgery and those who do it regularly know well what can happen if something goes wrong. Bruce stared back at Whitaker; he knew what this case would mean: the opening of a skull that had been opened before for other procedures, sliding the brain gently backward, implanting part of a rib bone at the back of the eye socket to prevent the dura's future intrusion. Under the best of circumstances, it would be dangerous. And this was not the best of circumstances. Not with all the scar tissue that was sure to be there, carrying with it the possibility of adhesions. Not with the blood losses that were mounting.

Whitaker was insistent.

Katowitz listened to Whitaker and said, "I agree with you. We ought to do it now."

But Bruce, a Scotsman who was known for his boldness, his willingness to try procedures that others would not try, did not agree. It would be, after all, his responsibility. And in his opinion, a craniotomy for Lisa was too risky, even for the likes of Derek Bruce.

"This is the day to do things," Whitaker said impatiently. "I don't want to slip back to just doing minimal things because minimal things have already been tried and they haven't done anybody any good."

"Up until now, you've been working with just the soft tissue," Bruce replied. "We haven't done anything that is really life-threatening. The loss of some skin over a skull that's intact isn't so big a problem, even if it becomes superficially infected. But if we do a craniotomy, we'll be exposing the intracranial space to the infection. And if we lose skin flaps and we have open bone down below, we'd have a direct communication with the brain and we'd be increasing the risks of meningitis. I'm not at all sure we can do what we want to do without opening that lining around the brain."

He was afraid that two membranes might have fused and that the dura might, in fact, be fused to whatever was at the back of her eye socket.

"I know this is going to tax both the patient and all of us, but better now than later," Whitaker argued. "I want to avoid major operations later on. I want to do this today."

They discussed it, heatedly, for about five minutes. At 1:05 P.M., Lecky ordered two more units of whole blood; Lisa was bleeding a great deal. Five minutes later, the craniotomy began. Ten minutes after that, Lecky called for two more pints of blood.

"It's a torrent of bleeding," sighed one of the doctors who were observing.

Bruce attached a fiber-optic light to his head. With a drill, he made three holes in her head: one in the front, over the base of the middle of the forehead, another over the end of where the sphenoid wing should have been, just behind the eye, then a third on top of the head.

With thin, delicate instruments, Bruce began to retract the dura, and the brain within it, out of the way. He was actually moving a brain, pushing it aside, gently.

Bruce had done this sort of thing before; craniotomies are not rare. But what if, as he suspected, there were adhesions? Suppose, as a result of past surgeries, two surfaces had joined when they should have remained separate? It happens when scar tissue forms and if it had happened in this case, he might penetrate the dura. He wanted to avoid that at all costs.

But there were no adhesions. The three holes were joined, a piece of skull bone was lifted off, a piece of rib bone was inserted where the sphenoid wing should have been, and the whole thing was put back together again.

"It was easier than I thought," Bruce said, as he left the operating room in mid-afternoon.

"I know I'm going to survive it and that eventually it will work out," Lisa had said. "When I was three they said I wouldn't live to see four. I don't like myself very much and I don't know what I want, except I want to be treated like a human being."

Whitaker went back to finishing her new nose. He stared at the bits of her rib bone obsessively, like a determined little boy making a scale model of something very important to him. He had already removed the old nose by making an incision across the rim of it, turning up a flap of skin and removing everything between the dermis, the inner layer of the skin, and the cartilage and bone underneath. The rib grafts were V-shaped, like nasal bones. Set where the old nose was, the skin was pulled over the graft and the new nose was in place.

By 2:25, she had been given 21 units of whole blood; 20 units of platelets, the tiniest of elements in blood, which tend to stick to surfaces that have been damaged; 3 units of blood plasma and 750 cubic centimeters of albumin. Her blood volume had been replaced approximately four times. By 3:10, Jantzen was noting that Lisa had received 24 pints of blood, 4 liters of saline, 10 units of platelets and 10 units of plasma.

Through all of this, Whitaker had not left the operating room, had not stopped working, even once. The only time he sat down was when he fashioned the new nose. And now he was back on his feet, inserting and implanting what he had made under the skin that had always been there; skin he had saved during the removal of tumor, skin that could be stretched and used again.

Observers who watched the entire operation were by now experiencing a tiredness that was, in itself, painful. The pain of standing started in the heel, worked up the back of the leg, rendering the calf putty in transit, and finally attacked the thighs frontally. Then it moved to the low back, gnawed into shoulder muscles and finally marched up the back of the neck.

"It's easier to work than to watch," Whitaker told them.

At around four o'clock, Lisa's face was beginning to swell up, but not so much that one could not see the new nose, the presence of a profile, at last, and no more tumor. In her repose, she looked curiously like a baby. The blood loss slowed, then stopped. The cauterization had finally worked. She received her 35th pint of blood at about 5:00 o'clock. By the end of it, which came at between 5 and 6, she received 20 units of whole blood, 15 units of packed red cells, 10 units of fresh frozen plasma, 750 cubic centimeters of albumin, 420 cubic centimeters of a saline solution, 800 cubic centimeters of the dextrose solution. Lisa's blood loss as measured by the scores of sponges that were weighed before and after use was estimated at 6,000 cubic centimeters, but as Jantzen explained to me later, Lisa lost a lot of blood that could not be measured accurately because it left her so quickly. In the next two days, she would receive another two pints of blood.

After more than eight hours, it was over. Lisa had gotten a new face and she would live. But what kind of face would it be and what kind of life?

I asked Whitaker that evening what he thought the future held for Lisa now.

"I think that she will feel very different about herself . . . she will start to have some positive feelings. It will come from the little things that don't happen as opposed to what used to happen. There should be a lack of negatives. She'll look in the mirror one day and she'll have different feelings."

Chapter Thirteen

The next morning, I was particularly eager to talk to Derek Bruce. I had seen the craniotomy but it came unexpectedly, somewhat for him and very for me. Why hadn't they seen the pulsating eye before?

Bruce, who retained just a shade of a gentle burr he had brought with him from his native Scotland, thought it was "good luck" that he had been able to do the craniotomy so uneventfully, and he was clearly relieved that the dura had not been penetrated.

The sudden discovery of the pulsing right eye had fascinated him, even though it caused him to do an operation he had not wanted to do.

"I think we didn't notice it before," he said, "because of so much soft tissue in that area and so we saw the orbit of the eye poorly. We didn't see enough of the eyeball to appreciate it."

Lisa's brain, or at least the protective dura around it, actually had been pressing against the eye's orbit. It was difficult to accept: the precious, inviolable brain, an organ of such power that it cannot be ever thought of as exposed or vulnerable. But here was the brain deprived of true sanctuary, with the result that it appropriated the space of the eyes and thus damaged the eyes—whose images it computed, assessed, considered in the mystery of billions of nerve cells.

Bruce took out a picture of Lisa's CT scan and somebody else's CT scan, for comparative purposes.

In one scan, the sphenoid wing could be seen quite clearly. That is the way it would look for most people. The orbit of the eye was separate, the brain was totally contained within the cranial cavity.

But with Lisa's scan, the bone simply wasn't there. There was literally nothing to keep the dura, bearing its soft and pinkish gray treasure, from intruding into the back of the eye's orbit. In Lisa's case it had intruded but now that was fixed with a piece of bone taken from her ribs.

"It won't change her vision," Bruce said of the bone transplant, "but perhaps it will prevent her remaining eye from working its way out and, in the long run, it may preserve what vision she has."

Why was the sphenoid wing missing? Had the neurofibromatosis destroyed it?

Bruce thought not. The bone barrier had probably been missing since birth and it was just another dimension to the mutation that had caused the neurofibromatosis. Her genetic code had thus given her the growth of tissue that she did not need, but cheated her out of a bone that she did need.

Katowitz, whose office was near Bruce's, dropped by and told us he was about to depart for a visit to intensive care and he asked me if I'd like to accompany him.

We found her at one end of the intensive care room, which was protected with a tight security guard. Lisa's story, now made public, had generated much interest among Philadelphia's journalists, as well as those in other parts of the country. The hospital was surprised at the unprecedented extent of the interest and, although it wanted to cooperate with reporters, it couldn't have them barging into intensive care. One of them, a broadcaster whose audacity had overpowered his judgment, had already tried to gain entry by posing as a doctor, one guard told us. The guards were suspicious. Katowitz, understandably, had a bit of trouble getting me in. For a brief time, they even suspected that he was a reporter.

Lisa's bed had a screen in front of it. She seemed quite alert. She already knew that the big tumors were gone and that she had a different face now. But even if someone had given her a mirror, she could not have begun to determine what she looked like, any more than we could, looking at her. Her face was badly swollen and the work that Whitaker and Katowitz had done was lost, temporarily, in the classic reaction of tissue to surgical steel. She couldn't speak, either, because the endotracheal tube that enabled her to breathe was still in place.

She could hear, though, and she squeezed Katowitz's hand when he told her that he was very pleased with the results.

"You're wonderful," Katowitz whispered in her ear.

Lisa shrugged her typical shrug, making it clear, as was her habit, that she didn't think she was wonderful. After all, she hadn't done the surgery. They had.

Katowitz entered his observations in a report; the intensive care nurses assured him she was doing well.

Katowitz's job, no less than Whitaker's, had been extremely difficult. With the left eye removed, a prosthesis would soon be put in place that would be the size of and look quite a bit like a normal eye. But with the right eye remaining and greatly enlarged, it would be impossible to approach symmetry.

Katowitz knew that he had to strive for a measure of symmetry anyhow, because Lisa's eyes, like the eyes of any woman or man, would be noticed first. The eyes were the anchor for the rest of the face. It was impossible to tell for sure what he had achieved. That would reveal itself very slowly only over a period of months. Still, he could make some preliminary judgment.

"I am happy with what we were able to do with the eyelids," he said, once we were out in the hall. "You recall how huge her eyelids were—just about twice the size of normal eyelids. I thinned out as much of the tumor as I could along the lids so as

157

to create lid creases. Now, her eyes will be more almond shaped."

He said that her eyes were made a bit more slanted because the narrower fissure would give her more protection and, he hoped, be more aesthetically appealing.

He made plans to give her a temporary prosthesis in the left eye. Indeed, the first thing Lisa asked him when she could speak was, "When do I get the prosthesis?"

Once people learned of Lisa's story, they sent her many hundreds of letters. I ultimately read each letter carefully, looking for evidence of the people who had punished her for so many years.

But no such people wrote. It seemed as if the people whose view of the world had been so dominant in public places had been replaced by quite another species.

Conspicuous among them were those who shared her interest in Bach.

A retired New York State civil servant, now resident in the Torrington, Conn., Y.M.C.A., wrote:

"Ever hear Bach's *Magnificat*? It is a truly yummy piece: a wonderful circus of everything; and you can kind of climb inside it, wrap it around you and cuddle down. What really turns me on is that, even though I am on the way toward being sixty—terribly OLD, huh?—I know that there's an enormous amount of Bach's music that I've never heard yet. And, since I plan to live happily to about 125 years old or so, it is wonderful to be able to count on not running out, you know?"

Then he added: "People are not all rotten, ya know, kid. Lots of good Joes out here in the bushes."

Bach lovers also responded with music, sending Lisa enough records and tapes to impress many FM stations.

She received no fewer than four versions of the St. Matthew Passion; all of the concertos for harpsichord; all of the cantatas; the Brandenburg Concertos; the Goldberg Variations; a *Magnificat* or two; lots of music for violin, including the "Chaconne" from the Violin Partita no. 2; an awesome amount of organ music; and lots of shorter things for all manner of instruments.

There was unavoidable duplication. Months later, an understanding record shop near her home let her exchange duplicates for music she did not have.

With all of it, she never did discard the grocery store Brandenburg Concertos no. 2 and no. 6.

Other writers were no less caring.

A man from Pennsylvania's Lehigh Valley wrote: "Here is a small donation [he sent her ten dollars] that I want you to use for something you will enjoy—not for medical expenses. I would send more but being retired for nine years it is difficult to make ends meet. Having seen so many disfigured and mangled people as an ambulance attendant, I am so grateful that you are being helped for something which you could not control. . . ."

And there were letters from people who had severe handicaps of their own.

"I too was born with a congenital disorder," wrote one of them, "and have gone through a lot of surgery in my lifetime. I am getting old now but I did have a happy life with a good husband and two children. There is a bright future and much happiness for you. . . ."

Quite a number of other neurofibromatosis victims wrote, as did people with no handicaps at all, who felt she helped them put their lives in better perspective. One of them, an inmate in Trenton State Prison, advised Lisa to "cleave to faith."

A Philadelphia woman wrote, "I must sin a lot when I complain of a headache or when my hair doesn't look just so when I go out. I must promise myself to thank God for what I have."

If there had been children who had feared her as a monster, then there were also children in the fifth grade at St. Joseph's School in Niagara Falls, N.Y., who told her they wanted to be kept notified of how she did. And students in the Allen W. Roberts School in New Providence, N.J., sent her a huge handmade get-well card. One boy wrote, "You deserve a 21-gun salute. Bang. Just open this card 20 more times."

If her peers had shunned her, there were multiple offers of friendship from people from all walks of life. A young woman in nearby Camden, N.J., a student at Camden Community College, offered to be a pen pal and even sent along a stamped, self-addressed envelope if she wanted to reply; a physician in New York City suggested that if she had not yet seen the play *The Elephant Man* (she hadn't), she ought to consider seeing it. He said if it were revived and she wanted to go, he'd be glad to take her.

A boy of nine years in Manhattan told her, "Whoever makes fun of you should be ashamed of themselves. . . . I am sending five dollars of my money so that you can buy classical music witch [sic] you like or spend it on anything els [sic]."

A girl, also nine years old, said, "If I knew you real good I would be your best friend."

A judge of the Ninth Judicial District in Carlisle, Pa., also sent her a check with the suggestion, "Put this toward the prettiest dress you can find." His sentiments that Lisa spend her money for something other than medical costs were echoed repeatedly.

A junior at the University of Pennsylvania said, "I am presently . . . deciding what future profession to pursue. I had always thought that I would be a medical doctor, but recently the pressures of school had made me re-evaluate my desire for a medical career. However, after reading about your problem . . . my career anxiety pains may just have been cured. The physical and psychological relief which your doctors can give you woke me up to understand just why I wanted to be a doctor. So, I thank you for helping me get through a difficult decision. And good luck to both of us in the future."

A Roman Catholic priest in Shortsville, N.Y., sent her his prayers and some money ("People are very good to their pastor at Christmas time and I would like to share my gifts with you," he said) and told her: "If you ever come to the Finger Lakes country you and your family are as welcome as the Lord Himself."

There were all kinds of prayers from all kinds of people.

"The burdens some must bear in life are almost beyond belief," wrote a woman from St. Louis, Mo. "Who, then, are we ever to complain about anything?" Then followed a little prayer in Hebrew, to which the woman added, "I know God hears the prayers of a Jew, too."

"I am not a believer in God," wrote a man from Brooklyn, "but if there is a deity or some such divine power, may its healing grace be yours." He signed it, "Yours in hope, concern, admiration and love."

Lisa's circumstances touched all kinds of people. Among them, Tatiana Troyanos of the Metropolitan Opera, who wired her a good luck message the night before her surgery. And Yoko Ono, whose husband, John Lennon, had been murdered only a year before, sent Lisa a crystal box and his album, "Double Fantasy."

Howard Gordon, director of Macmillan Book Clubs, said that, "As a former librarian . . . I don't have to tell you that I think people who read should inherit the earth." He offered to send her books on any subject she chose and closed with, "I'll be disappointed if you don't ask for books."

One writer said, simply, "Thank you for being."

Mary and Diane read all the letters and cards carefully, and read most, if not all of them, to Lisa after her release from the hospital more than a month later. Although Lisa's eyesight was sharply impaired and deteriorating, she hand-wrote a response, which was then duplicated by a Catholic church. Her note said, "Just writing 'Thank you.' Can never fully express my gratitude toward you, my kind new friend. I want you to know how happy you made me. Thank you and God bless you, too." Lisa was never entirely happy with the card because when she wrote it, her handwriting, affected by her vision, was shaky.

Nor was she able to respond to everyone who wrote to her, although she had wanted to and Mary and Diane helped her. The letters suggested that many of the writers believed she had managed to control her problems in one big, dramatic event.

Unfortunately, it was not to work out that way.

Chapter Fourteen

Over the next twenty-one months, Lisa underwent four more operations on her face. That brought her lifetime total of operations on her face and on her head to sixteen—one surgery for every seventeen months of life.

These later procedures were not as daring as the effort of December 9, 1981. They did not take nearly as much time. They did not involve anywhere near the same blood loss. But there was blood loss—more blood than anyone wants to lose. There was pain—more pain than anyone wants to feel. But the operations were important, both to Lisa and to her doctors.

In January of 1982, about a month after the big operation and shortly before her release from the hospital, Whitaker and Katowitz found that she needed some new skin grafts. Some of the skin flaps that had been applied the month before showed signs of necrosis, or cell death, because of inadequate blood supply to the flaps. Katowitz also gave her a skin graft on part of the right upper eyelid in an effort to lower it a bit. The skin for the graft came from behind an ear.

In May of 1982, only five months afterward, Whitaker removed a deformed portion of the mucosa of the lip and reshaped the rest.

He also did more work on the nose in an effort to remove some bulkiness and thus enhance her profile. He also worked to give her nostrils more shape. From her groin, he took some dermis, the fibrous inner layer of the skin, to fill in a depression along the right side of her head, caused by the removal, the previous December, of tumor. He removed more neurofibromas, small ones, most specifically on the left mandible along the jaw line. Finally, he gave her a new chin with an implant made of a kind of silicone. The larger chin and more chiseled nose gave her a better profile and made her head look somewhat smaller.

In the same procedure, Katowitz removed scar tissue from the orbit of the enucleated left eye; reduced thickness of eyelids; and created a new angle for her eyelids so as to achieve a symmetrical look. The lids had an overcorrected upward tilt to them now, evocative of Asian eyes, because it was assumed that, after surgery, they would gradually drop lower by themselves.

In February of 1983, fourteen months after his first surgery on her, Whitaker operated again to make the chin still bigger and thus gave her a larger implant; removed some tissue from the inside of the left side of the mouth; took a dermis graft from her left side and transplanted it to her right temporal region; took some fascia lata, which is tissue from the left thigh area, and used it to support a corner of the mouth; decreased the tilt of the eyes on each side (they did not droop as expected, after surgery, because of the unpredictable quality that neurofibroma infiltration had given to her skin); and, finally, removed bumps from the left jaw line where he had excised tissue before.

In October of 1983, Whitaker and Katowitz operated a fifth time, refining and correcting the shape of her eyelids and excising tissue from some of the lumpier areas still left on her face.

Her family and friends—including Verna Mitros—watched the operations come and go, first in absolute wonderment, then apprehension, then a dreadful resignation. They could not believe that she was subjecting herself to so much for what they thought would now be very modest returns. Whitaker had said that he had already done ninety-five percent of all that he could do, all of what was possible, and he repeated that her face would never be totally "normal." Her face, as a result of all this work, was substantially improved. But it still did not look like everyone else's face. Family members asked her to consider stopping the surgery or at least postponing it.

"My family is upset with me because they don't understand," Lisa said. "They don't understand that I have to do this. I want to do it and want to get it done with as quickly as possible. I know this hurts them more than it hurts me."

To Lisa, even a tiny amount of improvement in such a face was better than nothing, and so the girl who always took a pain killer when she went to the dentist and regarded herself as quite sensitive to pain was subjecting herself to a great deal of it.

After Whitaker's first operation, Lisa did not even try for many months to look at herself in the mirror because she wanted to wait until most or all of the swelling went down. Still, Diane recalls that her sister would unavoidably catch glimpses of herself when she washed her face and brushed her teeth.

With so many operations coming so quickly, there is a question as to whether what she saw was, in fact, a final product, a face that would be hers from now on. It takes months after major plastic surgery for the face to assume the shape it is going to have. Even after the swelling goes down, some tissue readjustment occurs.

Diane was with her when she did look at herself closely for the first time, but it was uneventful. Lisa looked, nodded, did not react very strongly one way or the other. At that point there had already been a tremendous metamorphosis. And yet, she said nothing.

As she recuperated, she put herself on a diet, suppressing her yen for Peanut Chews and sugar in whatever form it might take, and lost around thirty pounds. She bought a wig, then another wig, then still another, then a couple of bikinis and some very nice dresses. She always bought things to fit her neatly and precisely at her thinnest so that she would have a reason not to slip back into her old eating habits. The diet and the new clothes pleased her family because they knew that she knew she looked better. But dieting and scheduling operations at the same time do seem inappropriate to each other, they told her.

"I have to do this," she said. "I'm still not happy with the way I look."

But how good could she look? What more should Whitaker realistically be trying to do for her?

"I never know how to quantify questions like that," he said. "When people ask me how much improvement there is going to be on a nose, what is an end point? About the best I can do in answering that is that she will have things that would identify as a normal relation of structures. Her eyes will tilt up properly, her nose will have some projection and some definition of a profile. You should be able to see her cheekbones and her chin will be better. But she still won't look 'normal.' Part of it will be the immobility of her face, because of the nerve injuries, some of it will be just because of the character of her skin, and some of it will be because of the scars."

Whitaker talked about the "structure, proportion and harmony" that he wanted to create in Lisa's face. Would the fine-tuning ultimately be worth it to her?

"You know what drives her," he said. "She knows without ever verbalizing it that the majority of people will never get behind her face. And even those of us who do get behind it, have to compensate for her face in our own brains. Sad to say, most people can't deal with that. They can't make the compensation. They put up a defense, they start teasing her and then they say offensive things because they don't know what else to say. If they would only try to look behind her face, I think they would all find her appealing. That's what's happened at the hospital. Everybody who got to know her liked her and more or less forgot her face."

There was thus a covenant between Lisa and Whitaker. He had given her his surgeon's promise that he would make her look as good as his skill allowed. And she had promised herself that she would do whatever it took to achieve the best result.

They both knew that the marvel within the sum total of a face is its detail, the smallest particles of what is probably the most compelling universal mosaic we know. Whatever the result, she was entitled to take the chance. And under the circumstances, Whitaker had to offer it to her.

Quite aside from the aesthetics involved, there were medical reasons for doing more. The gross removal of tumor and the creation of a new face created inevitable needs that could not be anticipated before surgery. For example, she had some trouble breathing through her new nose. Its interior had to be corrected.

Yet, when Lisa told Diane that she was going to have yet another surgery—the third one Whitaker would do—Diane burst into tears. And Mary began to think that perhaps Lisa was caring less about life itself than she ought to. She seemed to grow compulsive about conquering her neurofibromatosis and more distant toward her family.

At one point, Jennifer confronted her.

"I told her, Lisa, I said, there were a couple of scares after each of these last two operations and she told me that she didn't care. She said, if he [Whitaker] says he can do something for my face, something to make my face better, I'm going to have it done. I said to her, how can you feel that way? I said, you've been under too much anesthesia. I said, what you've been under in one year, most people aren't under in their whole lifetimes. I told her that I didn't think her body could take all that abuse.

"I think she'd rather die on the operating table," Jennifer added. "That would be easier for her. That's why she's willing to go on with these things. I told her, you're giving us all heart failure, you're killing us, too. You have to understand that when the thing is over and then there's a crisis, we all die a million times. But she just told me I didn't understand.

"If she would be more public about who she is, it might be better," Jennifer said. "Sometimes, I think, if she would only let in the people who really care. She needs people. She needs people to invite her to their house for lunch, she needs people who want to take her for day trips, people who are not her family. That's what the hell she needs. She does what she does because she's scared of people. She'll say, 'Well, they're just doing that because they feel sorry for me' and I say yes, they do feel sorry for you, but also, they really, really care."

The sweep of surgery was difficult to consider but there were several other things at work now that had nothing to do with surgery. She was twenty-one years old, soon to be twenty-two. Like most others of that age, she was trying to establish her own identity and some independence. Some abrasiveness developed between Lisa, her mother and her sisters, but they understood it. They had all been twenty-one themselves and what she said and how she acted in many respects reflected what they themselves had done.

But unlike them, Lisa could not establish or even totally define the independence she sought. Her vision was getting worse and her continuing effort to obtain a new face made it inevitable that she would remain at home and live as she had lived all of her life—with her parents. Her family understood that, too, and told me so many times. They also knew that there was something else going on in Lisa.

"Nobody knows what to do for her," Mary told me in a telephone conversation. "Nobody knows what to do with her. This is not our Lisa. Not the Lisa we know. It isn't anger she feels, it's hurt. She says, 'Why doesn't he give me a break?'"

"Who is *he*?"

"She meant God. She wants to know when God is going to give *her* a break. She gets so upset over these kids who still make fun of her."

One day during this period, Lisa and Mary were in Woolworth's and there were two small boys sitting in a shopping cart, waiting for their mother.

One boy looked at Lisa, turned to the other boy and said, "Did you see her face?"

Lisa heard him, walked back to where they were, looked at them and said, firmly but gently, "Did you see your face?"

167

Another day, Lisa, her mother and Aunt Gert were out together and a little boy came up to Lisa, yanked on her sleeve and said, "Hi."

Aunt Gert walked Lisa off in one direction and Mary looked sternly at the little boy and said, "Who are you?" It turned out he was Joey Amato, aged 9, the son of a neighbor of Diane's and a friend of Lisa's. Not a tormentor at all.

There was the time that Lisa was with Diane in a branch of Abraham & Straus near Philadelphia. A little boy came up.

"Hi," he said to Lisa. "What's wrong with you?"

"Nothing," Lisa replied. "What's wrong with you?"

Diane said, "Well, do you want me to kick him?"

"No, let's just go."

Lisa had received, the previous Christmas, a book entitled *Art Treasures of the Vatican* from Howard Gordon of Macmillan Book Clubs.

"This is a beautiful book," Mary said. "It has big pictures, and he even sent her books with large print and she was really very happy. You know how she loves to read. But now, I see there's another thing that's got her unhappy. She can't read the book. She can't *see* the book. I don't think she can even see herself in the mirror. You know what she does? She listens to television. That's what she does. She *listens*."

"She's down, way down," Arlene said. "I said from the beginning, and nobody liked me for saying it, that she should have gone to a special school. She needed a structure away from the family to learn to cope and to learn to be.

"Now she's sick and she doesn't know who to turn to. She's blocking out just about everyone. I asked her last night if she wanted to go camping and she just said, 'Nope.'"

Lisa was insistent that nobody make her situation appear worse than it really was. Once, for example, Diane told some people that Lisa had been denied a job because of the way she looked. Lisa angrily denied that and said the prospective employer was willing to hire her for an office job but that she had to turn the job down because she did not have transportation. She had never bothered to tell Diane what really happened.

In the months between operations, after the swelling had gone down, Lisa could see that she looked better. Whitaker took photographs and studied her face closely every few months, looking for some indication of growback. There was none.

But even those who agreed she looked better did not always spare her the public displays she loathed.

One day in Strawbridge's, for example, a saleswoman ran up to her and said, "Oh, I'm so happy for you," and started to cry. The saleswoman was a friend of Mary's.

She apologized for crying, emphasized her happiness, but told Lisa: "You have a way to go yet."

On the same shopping trip, Lisa took Diane's Lara (then ten years old) into a shopping center bookseller's to buy a Nancy Drew mystery.

Someone screamed, papers at one end of the store flew into the air and a woman ran to Lisa and embraced her.

"Oh, I hope you don't mind," she said. "I hope you don't mind me making such a fuss."

"I guess she knew my mother, too," Lisa said later. "Everybody knows my mother."

It became harder for Lisa to keep her patience. She said that she was growing tired of being polite, tired of going the other way to avoid possible tormentors.

"I still get aggravated when they do that to me, it still hurts but it makes me angry," she said. "I don't know. I think I have gone from being a Goody Two-shoes little mouse to being a bitch and I really don't like either one. I think that maybe everybody expects too much of me."

At one point, she seemed to be on an alarming emotional slide, in marked contrast to the optimism she had shown just six months before.

"I'm not angry, I'm disgusted," she said. "I'm tired. People are afraid of anybody or anything different. It isn't just me. It's my friends, too, my friends who are oddballs. Look at what they did to Bobby."

She was asked if she could accept the fact that she was different and that there were people who would accept her and people who would not accept her.

"I know I'm a freak," she said. "I'm saying that I'm a freak and that's how everybody sees me. Not everybody. Correction. A small number of people may not see me that way but most do. People tell me I should accept the fact that I'm different. I know I'm different. I accept it."

Mary reported a conversation she had with Lisa about then.

"She said to me, 'I don't know whether I got that much out of it.' She said, 'They took my eye, they took my sight and they took my hair and so what did I get out of it?' She's talking about the most essential thing in a woman's life, right? She said, 'People only take you for the way you look, not for the way you are. They only take you for the way you look and they take one look at me and they don't want to be bothered with me.'"

Lisa had been classified as "legally blind" for years, although she could always see well enough to read and to walk and do many other things. But now she was losing much of the sight that remained in her right eye. A cataract in that eye grew more formidable and she had to consider whether she wanted to risk a surgery for the cataract's removal. Under ordinary conditions, a cataract operation is not so serious. But this eye was her only eye and it had been operated on years before. It contained fluid, scar tissue, obstacles that would make surgery more difficult. "I think we can get a good result," Katowitz said, adding, "but it's her only eye."

In a letter to me, he summarized her situation:

"Blindness is not really the correct term [to describe her condition]. She is having difficulty, probably due to cataract formation. Her pressure is now controlled and she can still function, i.e., walk around without assistance. But she has more bad days then good when she can't read.

"I have carefully placed the decision for cataract surgery in her hands. She now has only one eye and that eye has had many procedures. I do believe that with our modern micro-surgical instruments we can remove the cataract safely.

"But the risks of complication or even loss of the eye itself are still present. I have told Lisa to think about all of this and to let me know when she feels that her life is being compromised to the point that she wants to take that risk. Then we will suck out the cataract with a fine needle-type instrument.

"How much vision she will then have will depend not merely on the success of the procedure but also on the extent of the damage that glaucoma has created in the past and the continuing pressure of the gliomas [tumors] in her right orbit which are attached to the optic nerve.

"The decision is Lisa's. It is easy for me to say I would do it now. But would I really risk losing even the sense of daylight in the morning—or the sense of dusk to evening? We take so much for granted. Lisa will let us know."

Postoperative depression is not uncommon. The question was whether Lisa's was too severe for too long.

At one point, a friend of Lisa's mentioned her predicament to Penny Aviles, a warm and engaging woman in her early forties who lived in New York and who worked closely with the National Neurofibromatosis Foundation there. Her own neurofibromatosis was serious, with dozens of tumors covering half of her face as well as elsewhere on her body. Her case might be called a typically severe one, yet in terms of the damage it had done to her face, it was not nearly as bad as Lisa's, where the tumors were much larger and covered both hemispheres. Penny wore a patch over one damaged eye.

Like Lisa, she had experienced much shunning. She would make an ideal adviser and she was asked if she would meet with Lisa. She readily agreed, but Lisa wouldn't see her.

"I can't handle that right now," she said.

Since the big operation, Lisa had been taking acetazolamide, one of the older, more reliable diuretics, frequently prescribed for relieving pressure in the eyes of certain types of glaucoma patients. Katowitz had prescribed it for Lisa because it would tend to reduce the amount of fluid secreted into her remaining eye. He was still trying to control the glaucoma that had first plagued her when she became Scheie's patient, years before, a problem nobody had been able to solve.

But even a proven drug given by an alert specialist for a very good purpose can have unwanted side effects. According to several sources, including the American Medical Association Drug Evaluations, acetazolamide may cause "dizziness, confusion and depression" in some patients. Lisa had all three symptoms but her confusion about what was happening to her made it all but impossible for her to tell them clearly and emphatically enough what was happening.

Finally, she summoned the wherewithal to tell Katowitz, "I think that if I take any more of it, I won't be able to get out of bed."

He did not want to lose its pressure-lowering advantage completely and so he tried to give it to her in a different form and then in a lower dose. She was finally taken off it completely and switched to another medication. Less than two weeks after she stopped taking the suspect drug, the depression appeared to abate and started to evaporate.

But nobody could say for sure how much had been the medicine talking and how much the medicine had been only the vector for releasing what was really in her soul.

Lisa now had a new life to live, whether she could see and whether the disparagers who lurked in public places approved of her or not. How would she live it and when would she begin?

Chapter Fifteen

C~~~~O

It would have been especially witless to expect Lisa to have undergone and overcome five operations within the span of two years, recover from all of them quickly, banish the shopping center carpers and their slams from her consciousness, then fully enjoy what the fates—and her surgeons—had given to her.

And yet neither her family nor her doctors could be blamed for hoping that she might somehow provide an inkling of how she felt about living in the present, dealing with the future and keeping the past where it belonged. That was only another example of why she thought some of them were expecting too much of her.

They wondered what she would do next week, next month, next year, and they worried about it.

Then, one day, they learned that Lisa had decided to start taking classical ballet lessons. About two months had passed since her fifth surgery under Whitaker's supervision, the bout with depression was even more recent than that, but she was going to learn the dance.

Her decision to study dance was the first strenuous physical activity she attempted after surgery.

Her vitality seemed to be returning; the ballet lessons represented a new foray in every sense of the word, a different kind of self-improvement. It took on a special significance because she had to pay for the lessons at a time when her own funds were quite meager. She could not have done such a thing as casually as someone who had ample discretionary income.

"It was Lara's idea," Diane explained. "But when Lisa heard about it she said she'd like to try it, too, and so I thought, what the heck, we'll all go—Lara, Lisa and yours truly."

The next Tuesday, the three of them appeared at a white stucco building in a small suburban Philadelphia community that housed a school of ballet. Actually, there were four of them. Diane's son, Danny, who was seven years old, went along for the ride and out of his more than idle curiosity about anything his sister, three years his senior, might be interested in.

They climbed two flights of stairs to find a fairly large room, mirrored on one side, with the traditional oak barre running alongside the mirror. There were dressing rooms down one hall-way. The passageway to them was covered by a blue curtain that had white swans on it. And there were some large win-dows, overlooking a quiet parking lot.

The three new dancers changed into black shoes, black stock-ings and black leotards. Danny waited to assume the role of spectator.

The instructor was a pleasant woman in her late thirties who soon found that Lara, even though she had inspired the others to come for lessons, was not at all interested in the discipline that accompanied studying the dance. This truth was apparent to all, belying the commitment implied by Lara's purple T-shirt, which bore images of graceful ballerinas on its front. In truth, Lara was much more interested, at least that afternoon, in talking to Danny. Or maybe in not letting him see her learn anything. She was excused.

Diane and Lisa continued the class together. They learned the first of the five positions of the feet, heels touching, the idea to make a straight line with the feet. That was not as easy as it looked.

At one point, the instructor noticed that Diane and Lisa kept changing positions, with Diane always seeing to it that Lisa was closest to the instructor.

"My sister has a little problem with her vision," Diane told her. "I think she'll be able to see better if she's closer to you." The instructor smiled.

They learned the exercises as a little record player played dreadful exercise music. The white swans were as close to Tchaikovsky as these three were going to get that afternoon. No Tchaikovsky—or Stravinsky or Poulenc. Dancers have to earn the right to hear Tchaikovsky when they work.

Lara never did earn the right to hear Tchaikovsky. There were too many other things for a ten-year-old to do. Diane dropped out, too. There were other things a young mother had to do, not the least of which was keeping an eye on Lara and Danny. But Diane would always be available to take Lisa to the ballet lessons as long as Lisa wanted to take them. Diane had always been available to take Lisa to so many places in the past and, the fates willing, she always would be available.

Lisa continued alone in private lessons. She learned the other positions of the feet. She learned the *plié*, the *battement tendu*, and *le cou de pied*, exercises for the feet and the legs and the body that would make her stronger, stronger physically, stronger in the way she would come to feel about herself.

Postscript

The kinds of problems Lisa has encountered are by no means limited to people who have neurofibromatosis. There are scores of serious illnesses that manifest themselves physically, with the result that a lot of people who read this are more familiar with Lisa's experiences than they would like to be.

This book was Lisa's book. It was not the author's intention to try to catalogue other serious illnesses or even to present all of the modest amount that is known about neurofibromatosis. There are many maladies that can maim and disfigure. Those trying to deal with such problems need a lot more understanding from those who are lucky enough to be free of them.

For example, there may be harsh effects from the malfunction of the pituitary gland. It can cause gigantism and dwarfism. It can also cause acromegaly, an enlargement of the head and hands. Such people have for too long been the objects of much scorn.

Greatly increased activity of the thyroid gland can cause exophthalmos, a bulging of the eyes, which some also find amusing. Epileptics and hunchbacks continue to receive special attention, and George Eliot and Victor Hugo notwithstanding, not always to their favor.

There are bone deformities causing more than five fingers to appear on each hand or more than five toes on each foot, and people with those conditions know what the social liabilities may be.

There is mongolism, there is blindness with a variety of causes, and there are a host of acquired deformities. Thalidomide, for example, was a tranquilizer that, when taken during pregnancy, caused children to be born with seriously deformed limbs. The drug was used in Germany, Great Britain and the United States until its sale was halted in the early 1960s. The children who were its victims are now adults, about Lisa's age.

Suffice to say that these problems and others rival the destructive power of neurofibromatosis and it is neither this book's intent nor its province to suggest that the genetic disorder shared by Lisa and by Merrick is the worst of them or that there is, in fact, one that is the worst. As Lisa always said, "It's all from where you're at."

More than half the people now alive in the United States will die of heart disease or cancer. And yet neurofibromatosis and some of the other medical problems described above are probably more irrationally feared, at least by some, because of what they may do to the body outwardly.

Heart disease continues to have a kind of respectability about it, popularly associated, as it is, with high-pressure jobs and rich foods. There remains a terrible stigma associated with cancer. Some of its victims still do not want to tell anyone that they have it, insisting that even if it kills them, it should not be made public in an obituary. This kind of stigma seems to be diminishing; too many of us are getting cancer for that not to be the case. And we are constantly learning more about its causes and, thus, ways to avoid it.

Part of the fear about neurofibromatosis is that so little is known about it. It remains largely an enigma to physicians and so it is frightening to everyone. But that should not make it less "respectable" than heart disease. And having it does not carry with it the expected mortality of either serious heart disease or many forms of cancer.

Joan Rudd and Felice Yahr are the president and executive director, respectively, of the National Neurofibromatosis Foundation in New York and have worked hard to break down irrational feelings about neurofibromatosis. Here are some of their principal concerns:

• It is unknown which gene or genes may cause the disorder. Until the gene is found and its structure determined, a chemical cure may be more difficult to achieve, although certainly not impossible. In theory, at least, it would be possible to block or alter the message the neurofibromatosis gene is sending to the body, causing it to grow tumors. But no modifying agent can be devised or even considered until the nature of the error in the gene is understood. Mrs. Yahr says that a major thrust of neurofibromatosis research now is to locate the gene or genes. Scientists suspect that the gene is located on the fourth chromosome—the same chromosome that contains the gene carrying Huntington's chorea, a disease that attacks the brain and nervous system.

• In those cases where there are no known carriers of the neurofibromatosis gene in a family and the disorder is the result of a genetic mutation, scientists are, at present, still unable to say what causes the mutation (or most other mutations, for that matter) or if there is something we could avoid that would preclude it. The neurofibromatosis gene seems especially susceptible to mutation. It is believed that half the people with neurofibromatosis are the first members of their families to have it. If that is so, these victims did not inherit the disorder but have it because of a mutation. Therefore, no family is immune to neurofibromatosis.

• The lack of a genetic marker for neurofibromatosis probably means that there are some undiagnosed cases. Nobody is sure of how many; at least 100,000 cases have been diagnosed in the United States. It is believed to occur about once in every 3,000 births. It is neither bound by nor intensified in a racial or geographic area, nor does it predominate in one sex.

• Some people have symptoms so mild that they go undiagnosed for years; they have no reason to call them to a doctor's attention. Only sixty percent have "significant disfigurement." Doctors define this as such physical impairments as many lumps on the skin or a deformed arm, leg or hand. But the other forty percent may have symptoms so minor that they are barely noticeable. Such patients are lucky to escape the disorder's potential for maiming. But without a diagnosis, patients may thus unwittingly pass the gene along to a child, where it may capriciously assert itself with great destructive power. Indeed, researchers know of cases where the first time a parent realizes that he or she has it, is when it has appeared in a severe form in a baby.

Neurofibromatosis is thus not the easiest malady to diagnose and doctors in small towns and remote areas who may see only few cases in their careers may have trouble recognizing it. The benchmark to look for is the appearance of six or more café-au-lait spots on the skin, each one half a centimeter or more in diameter.

The National Neurofibromatosis Foundation says that in most cases tumors do not manifest themselves until puberty. Other possible signs of the disease in children are an abnormal growth rate, one that is too fast or too slow; deformations of bone and problems with vision.

The unknown gene for neurofibromatosis is classified by geneticists as autosomal dominant. That means that whether a person has the gene through inheritance or through mutation, there is a fifty percent chance that it will be passed on to each and every child he or she may have. The risk is therefore the same in every pregnancy. These odds are the same whether the carrier is male or female.

The foundation is underfinanced but has recently been able to give $40,000 a year in seed money to researchers interested in trying to solve the riddle of this disorder. Most of the grants are less than $10,000. This is a very modest amount for research. But neurofibromatosis research stands to benefit from genetic research in other areas and from basic research in the neurosciences.

Mrs. Yahr and Mrs. Rudd receive many letters from people who have neurofibromatosis. These letters make it clear that, in addition to the abuse they receive, the patients are frequently confused or misled about the nature of their illness. It is also clear that many of them are isolated, perhaps the only person in a small town to suffer the problem.

The foundation has been able to organize chapters in a number of states, which serve to support and educate people about what neurofibromatosis is. Those chapters, and contacts within them, are as follows:

ARIZONA—Patricia Collins, 3837 East Devonshire, Phoenix, 85018.

CALIFORNIA—Rhonda Mahacek, P.O. Box 1566, El Toro, 92630.

FLORIDA—Jane Pugh, P.O. Box 270313, Tampa, 33688.

ILLINOIS—Stephen Cooper, 1403 South St., Geneva, 60134.

MASSACHUSETTS—Pat Krug, 21 Vine Rock St., Dedham, 02026.

MICHIGAN—Dick Mette, 244 Birch Hill, Rochester, 48063.

NEW JERSEY (NORTHERN PART)—Donna Oetinger, 271 Reichelt Road, New Milford, 07646.

NEW YORK (NORTHEASTERN PART)—Barbara Wellman, P.O. Box 117, Gallupville, 12073.

NEW YORK CITY—National Neurofibromatosis Foundation [National Headquarters], 70 West 40th Street, 10018. This is the best place to write for general information.

OHIO—Dolores Goldfinger, 3709 Donegal Drive, Cincinnati, 45236.

OREGON—Joy Ann Fitzgerald, 2311 Southeast Courtney Avenue No. 7, Milwaukee, 97222.

SOUTHEASTERN PENNSYLVANIA—William Baum, P.O. Box 203, Ardmore, 19003.

VIRGINIA-NORTH CAROLINA—Betsy Kincaid, P.O. Box 1063, Suffolk, Va., 23434.

METROPOLITAN WASHINGTON, D.C. (DISTRICT OF COLUMBIA, NORTHERN VIRGINIA AND MARYLAND)—Mary Ann Wilson, 3401 Woodridge Court, Mitchellville, Md., 20716.